D1595477

THE BRILLIANCE OF THE COLOR BLACK

Through the Eyes of Art Collectors

Charles Moore

The Brilliance of the Color Black Through the Eyes of Art Collectors

Published by PETITE IVY PRESS
NEW YORK, NEW YORK, U.S.A.

Library of Congress Control Number: 2021945686
MOORE, CHARLES, Author
The Brilliance of the Color Black CHARLES MOORE

ISBN: 978-1955496230 (Hardcover)
ISBN: 978-1955496223 (E-Book)

ART / American / African American
ART / Collections, Catalogs, Exhibitions / General

Cover Illustration by Deanna Luu
Cover Art by Tariku Shiferaw
Foreword by Storm Ascher

QUANTITY PURCHASES: Schools, companies, professional groups, clubs, and other organizations may qualify for special terms when ordering quantities of this title. For information, email info@petiteivypress.com

This book is printed in the United States of America.

Table Of Content

Foreword

When I first met Charles Moore, it became clear that we had similar goals to define Black historical legacy in art while staying true to our communities' needs. Before us connecting, I read The Black Market five times over during the pandemic, using it to stay connected with my understanding of what I know as the art world during a time of little to no interaction with the avatars of the arts community and the objects and ideas we create and protect. The book reassured me of my place as an artist, curator, gallerist, critic, and now collector in this ecosystem of Black contemporary art. Yet I was still burning with questions for Moore, who I had the privilege of interviewing at The Harvard Club Boston. The final question was, of course, "Will there be a follow-up to this book?" There, I was first introduced to his idea of The Brilliance of the Color Black in the Eyes of Art Collectors, which he began working on right after The Black Market was published. It would delve deeper for collectors who have embarked on the beginning stages he presented in—for those like me who were hooked but needed more to support and protect our investments in Black legacy. In my review of The Black Market, I wrote: "Capturing the multi-hyphenate nature of contemporary collectors and arts workers is its most important anecdote." So now, with this new continuation and expansion of establishing that anyone can be a collector by deciding to embark on contributing to history and legacy, Moore gives us the tools to show that Black art cannot be ignored or othered because of its embedded nature of the more remarkable human experience. This sequel provides further guidelines to categorize our multifaceted and constantly growing echelon of Black art. It can effortlessly link our contemporary explorations with a corresponding historical movement or term.

As Black collectors move through the motions of growing our collections and experiences in the art world, we are not to think of Black art as a separate world, but instead, the fuel for the entire art world. The Brilliance of The Color Black harnesses the importance for collectors to continue supporting the preservation of the Black experience because it reflects the experiences of all people. If we are steadfast in investing, protecting, and representing Black voices and expressions, we also strengthen art history as a whole. Charles Moore accomplishes this idea by taking us back to expression as a whole, not just art objects but spoken word, music, and film. From dissecting artistic explorations in the music industry such as the visual album, most notably, Kanye West's film, Runaway, to breaking down the symbolism and critical influences of Faith Ringgold's masterpiece Die, Moore continues to show how Black people have always helped push along with sociopolitical conversations through engaging their talents and harnessing other viewers' understanding of the world. With this guide to understanding our place within a larger scale of historical account, we can further our influence on investments, institutions, public art projects, and artists' careers—Black collectors can not only collect Black art but contribute the works to a grander context through prestigious institutions and gaining positions of power and influence. The individuals interviewed in this follow-up to The Black Market have been doing this work for a long time, but having them laid out in a perfect web gives us a more defined movement of the 21st century. Advisors, curators, financial analysts, museum board members, and beyond are all positions historically not expected to be held by Black people. And yet, there are great examples of these underrated supportive roles within the art world who, through these interviews, will inspire more people of color to hold their own and continue this multi-hyphenated journey. Figures such as Dr. Joy Simmons, Larry Ossei-Mensah, Lola West, and Demetrio 'Dee' Kerrison have prestigious experiences and connections that come from perseverance, research, and dedication as Black should be required of any notable figure looking to make a difference. The small and interconnected nature of the current Black art world will soon expand due to Moore's contributions to methods of inspirational research. The Brilliance of the Color Black Through the Eyes of Art Collectors rewrites the western art historical lens instead of dismissing it, which stands as a hopeful integration. Unlike the gatekeepers before us, we can engage all audiences with these narrative tools and be catalysts for change. Moore solidifies what is already true but had to be etched into the archive.

Introduction

O ut of all the tincts that can fill up a canvas, black exudes brilliance. Art is the sum of its components; the union of fragments and parts *becomes* the work of art, a work that in turn can evoke a particular feeling, pay homage to a culture, reference history, or create an atmosphere. Color is what we perceive when we view a particular wavelength of light being reflected from an object. When we see red, we see a reflection of the longest divination of light, and when we see violet, we see the shortest reflected; the object absorbs rather than reflects all other wavelengths.

Tinctures such as black and white—which aren't technically colors; white being a reflection of all wavelengths of light combined, and black being what we perceive when an object absorbs all the light—convey a myriad of meanings and are hailed by artists as some of the most impactful shades on the palette wheel. Black, in particular, has been described as the queen of them all by Pierre-August Renoir, with similar sentiments being echoed by artists such as Knowledge Bennett, Odilon Redon, and Alteronce Gumby. Gumby even asserts that black is the most unique and diverse of all the rays of light.

Black and white each evoke distinct moods or feelings, in large part due to the superficial connotations that humans have granted each. Even these connotations can vary across eras and cultures, and even between individuals depending on their unique life experience.

Particular shades, then, can evoke a similar mood or meaning in those viewers with similar cultural backgrounds, and artists can therefore use a shade to purposefully produce a particular feeling in the majority of their audience. Red, for instance, is often used to connote passion, romance, or anger, while yellow evokes optimism and green a sense of balance or peace (likely because of its association with nature's calming effects). Black and white particularly are some of the most impactful shades at our disposal, due to their extensive networks of associations across cultures and histories. In Western culture, for instance, black has for centuries been associated with grief and death due to the mourning dress tradition that originated in the Renaissance period. It is used in art to convey melancholy, grief, and death or funerary themes.

African and Asian cultures, in contrast, associate the bleached antipodean with mortality, while in western cultures white denotes innocence and purity, in large part due to matrimony and nascency traditions, strengthening the illusion of ideal perfection. Human experience assigns unique meaning to each shade, and artists can draw from those meanings to create meaningful and complex works of art. Artists can make an even more striking visual impact by subverting the expectations associated with a particular shade—for example, utilizing stygian tones in wedding scenes or resplendent whites in scenes of grief.

Black, in particular, has played a massive role in

the development of art through history, being the first pigment used by prehistoric artists on cave walls to depict hominid and mammalian figures. Numerous artists throughout history have cited black as the superior of all hues, not only in the strength of its purest form but also in its versatility. A plethora of shades and hues can be formed from combining multiple pigments excluding black, as proved by Mario Moore in his painting 'That Beautiful Color' in which a Black woman is depicted in all black, set against a dark background. This example encompasses the fact that it (black) can represent a vast accumulation, rather than just the absence of.

In addition to the role black has played in the art world throughout history, it was also the first—and is the most common—pigment used by printing presses, which revolutionized the world of writing and allowed the dissemination of literature and knowledge. Like art, literature evokes emotion and challenges the reader. The use of black pigment was both functionally and visually instrumental, making newspapers and books easy to read for a vast audience.

History is integral to art, be it visual or literary art, since colors, artistic traditions, and mediums can evoke myriad moods and meanings depending on the era and place. The accurate recording of human history plays a vital role in ensuring that this evocation is possible. Artists can draw on an array of historiographical materials to learn about and understand various histories and cultures, enabling them to accurately represent, or even to subvert, the traditions of these cultures and create meaningful art.

Art is not only an instrument with which to examine

and bring attention to the past, but also a way to record the present and pave the way for the future—in each period, cultural and societal events and attitudes shape the art that is created, and this is particularly true now, when the world is more open than ever to the discussion of societal issues. In this book, I'll explore the color black, in all of its shades and expressions, and in all of its artistic brilliance.

Cover Story

Tariku Shiferaw—Killing Me Softly (The Fugees) (2020)

Iremember when I got the call from Artis letting me know that I was awarded the curatorial fellowship grant in the summer of 2020. They asked me for a short bio, a headshot, and an image of a piece of art that describes my work. My first thought was, "Don't they know I've never curated anything?" I called up Tariku and asked his permission to use one of his paintings on my profile. I wanted *Killing Me Softly (The Fugees)*. New York–based artist Tariku Shiferaw has made a career of exploring the significance of mark-making. There's a physical and a metaphysical sense of this act (and of his work, for that matter): the marking of surfaces—the paint onto the canvas or multimedia object before him—and the marking of oneself onto unique spaces, thoughts, or even societies. Born in Ethiopia and raised in Los Angeles, Shiferaw recognizes the ineluctable obstructions that people of color face in moving to and living in the United States. He explains that critics, galleries, and museums have virtually erased Black artists from the pages of history.

I argued in *The Black Market* that, "as a microcosm, art museums represented a member-only group of elite institutions that lived by their caste systems. Many Black students, by virtue of their environment, struggled to find their way inside those seemingly impenetrable doors."

Shiferaw, who earned a BFA in 2007 from the University of Southern California and an MFA from the Parsons School of Design in 2015, currently participates in the Open Sessions residency program at The Drawing Center and serves as an artist-in-residence at the LES Studio Program. Shiferaw is well versed in art history; his art historical knowledge adds credence to his views as he pronounces that midcentury Black abstract painters along the likes of Norman Lewis, Ed Clark, Sam Gilliam, Frank Bowling, and Virginia Jaramillo lacked the recognition they deserved by virtue of societal mark-making—that is, by gatekeepers casting people of color by the wayside in art history. Critics, galleries, and museums have all played a role in this gatekeeping; the times, however, are quickly changing. Shiferaw, through his layered abstract canvases, seeks to showcase this. Shiferaw's mission mirrors my statement in *The Black Market*: "As we make our way through the twenty-first century, we must learn to navigate the growing art world—a space where Black creators and collectors have gained momentum, cemented their voices, and established themselves as central players in a previously white-dominated industry."

In this same vein, Shiferaw explores his own identity via abstract expressionism. This intentionality came to light when he crafted *One of These Black Boys* (2016), a piece featuring a black background marked by a series of vertical blue lines. Here, the artist sought to create an abstract painting that was entirely his own—a piece that wouldn't be mistaken for others' work. In making this piece, there was also a sense of reclaiming his identity with subtle yet striking messages that resonate with his idiosyncratic worldview. He claims that the moment viewers (and even his peers) see abstract art, they wonder why Black artists don't pay direct homage to their heritage—that is, why they don't create pieces showcasing Black bodies, African symbolism, or other unmistakable insignia. "I have always asked myself, *Yo, what does 'Black art' mean?*", Shirefaw discloses. Yet, as he learned from the renowned artist Jack Whitten, Black art is emblematic of the piece's talent, not of what is most apparent from the outside.

Shiferaw is deeply inspired by music and by color—by the multilayered black and blue hues, and by what these colors represent on his canvases. He explores what it means to make blues music, what it means—as the expression goes—to "have the blues", and what it means to gaze at the sky and take in the richness and serenity of the color. But again, there's a contrast here: beneath the superficial beauty of the sky, the world below is rife with conflict, atrocities, and the very reasons why people experience the proverbial "blues." Pair this with the concept of Black skin swelling into soft, blue bruises upon impact—the notion of being "black and blue" as a form of injury, if you will, both literally and metaphorically—and the artist's work takes on an entirely new undertone. Behind the black and blue paint, behind the solid backgrounds and the thick stripes, is a cultural rebirth, a juxtaposition of themes and colors, and an overwhelming resilience. (During our conversation, Shiferaw describes how hip-hop is blues music reincarnated and how this musical reemergence is in itself a form of resistance that's unquestioningly integral to the Black experience.) Shiferaw pairs his abstract creations with politically fueled titles that provide a new avenue of imbuing a work with a story evoked through his mark-making.

Shirefaw points to musicians Nas and Lauryn Hill's 1996 track of the same name as the inspiration for his 2016 piece entitled *If I Ruled the World (Nas)*. Nas's track illustrates a reality where an almost Afrofuturistic existence would be more conducive to Black bodies in America. "If I ruled the world/I'd free all my sons", states Nas in the song, and so both the musician and Shiferaw, in their respective media, reimagine a world without constraint for Black people living in an overwhelmingly White society. Just as Nas sings of ruling a world in which prisoners are freed from Attica and sent to Africa, Shiferaw paints an abstracted, mostly geometric picture portraying a similar sense of freedom, inspired mainly by the rapper's song.

Growing up in Southern California, Shiferaw explains that more of his White peers smoked weed than his Black ones, yet the latter were predominantly incarcerated. There's a sense of vulnerability that Black bodies cannot escape no matter how they move through American society. When regarded alongside Nas's hit song, Shiferaw's canvases, in expressing similar ideas, become a cover of sorts.

This brings us to Shiferaw's latest work: *Killing Me Softly (The Fugees)* (2020). Inspired by The Fugees' version of the renowned song, the result is captivating in its visual simplicity: it is an entirely white piece with a textured background and black horizontal stripes moving across the bottom half of the canvas. There are more faint marks underneath the top layer of paint—vertical black and red stripes, a splash of green, and other details that the viewer must examine closely to process in full. Once observers assess the complexity of those underlying layers, they might consociate the piece as a homage of sorts to David Hammons's African American flag, a distinctive and vivid emblem of the early 1990s. Shiferaw admits that he'd wanted to honor Hammons's flag for years, and yet he knew he would have to offer his take on the concept to provide an authentic commentary on the subject. "I just painted it," he admits.

Yet Shiferaw didn't include the flag's stars; instead, he replaced them with *X*s—and featured twenty-three of them rather than fifty. Referring to his recent black-and-blue flag series entitled *Flags of Us*, composed of pieces resembling the American flag, Shirefaw states that the stars simply didn't sit well with him. The artist marked the designated corner of the flag with glistening *X*s in the series, selecting the number twenty-three for two distinct reasons. The first of which, Shiferaw explains, is to showcase his admiration for NBA superpower Michael Jordan. Jordan, to the artist, is symbolic of excellence, of soaring beyond expectations. The athlete's jersey number touched him on an emotional level and exists today in Shiferaw's pieces as an image of the dreams so many people struggle to realize. The second reason for the twenty-three stars is linked to human DNA, and particularly to the male and female chromosomes and how they are represented both scientifically and societally. Shiferaw considered that the chromosomes resemble *X*s, each designated by a diagonal slash, with two chromosomes coming together to form an *X*. In humans, each cell features twenty-three pairs of chromosomes, or *X*s: the same number listed on Jordan's jersey.

Returning to *Killing Me Softly (The Fugees)*, the viewer may wonder about the artist's process. Unlike in the flag series, the underlying mark-making is less blatant than Shiferaw's earlier pieces but no less impactful. Shiferaw added the white paint as a base, placing the black stripes in a parallel fashion to represent bodies. Black and bold, working by way of reductive movements to mask the motion underneath—the ambivalence of Black identity in America, the cultural overshadowing of many groups in the United States, and the impact of self-directed expressionism. His work explores the idea of commoditization, specifically the commoditization of Black people and culture, which makes *Killing Me Softly (The Fugees)* all the more intriguing as a source of inspiration. With the layering of black lines atop the white background, those Black bodies can, in a sense, reclaim control. It's a stunning visual manifestation of the idea of transforming the system and overhauling how societal gatekeepers objectify, question, and negate the Black experience.

"When I make abstract paintings or installations or sculptural works, it's directly referring to that," says Shiferaw. Regarding the title of the piece, Shirefaw says that, no matter how much he contemplated other options, it was the only one that came to mind. The idea behind the work is that society is, in many ways, *killing* the Black experience—but it principally does so indirectly, such that the oppression can continue to persist under the radar. Shiferaw references Roman mythology and ancient history along with the Judaic tradition to explore the concept of betrayal: betrayal with a kiss of a lover, or perhaps of a friend. He sought to delve into the notion of looking into a person's eyes, connecting with or smiling at them, and creating a tense and uneasy situation that, left unaddressed, could crumble. The fact that the song for which the artist named his piece is of disputed origin only amplifies the intricacy of this theme, how we listen to music or observe visual art, and the way Black bodies exist in the United States today.

Yet, as Shiferaw explains, the message behind the piece is that Black bodies have perpetually been the backbone of the United States. As a first-generation American, he believes that African Americans have historically been punished for the nation's cultural shortcomings. "I partake in that because of my upbringing here in the hood and because of the way everyone that looks like us gets treated," he discloses. "But [make no mistake], those that have been here for generations have paid the price." These individuals have been overlooked, worked tirelessly, and ultimately commodified for their labor, their bodies, and their culture, and yet they've never seen the fruits of their efforts.

"Black lives have always operated in a very different way than mainstream America," says Shiferaw. This notion is integral to our conversation here. Moving forward, perhaps viewers will learn to absorb and work to change this reality—to shift these circumstances for future generations and allow Black bodies to reclaim agency at the societal level. Abstraction, one might argue, is only the beginning.

Chapter 1

Penetrating the Psyche of Artists through Literature

This timely review of selected books, poems, and essays showcases the literary contributions of writers from the span of over a century. It illustrates the way in which they enrich the arts, artists, and art collecting. The worldviews articulated by these writers answer some of our most pressing questions concerning the evolution of the Black psyche. Can life be viewed through a multifaceted prism, or is it still starkly black and white? What is the unfolding Black experience of the American dream over time? How have their realities honed their artistic sensibilities? What are the redemptive qualities within their experience for future generations?

Ask any person why they collect art, and you are likely to receive an almost unending variation of answers. In *The Black Market*, I wrote, "If it is meant for personal viewing, then the piece will immensely impact the buyer, and they must feel a strong connection to the piece that ultimately compels them to purchase it. If the piece is purchased for the enjoyment of other people, then the piece likely will not speak as much to the buyer, instead solely serving as a status piece."

Some collect because of the financial value they perceive in certain art pieces. For others, it's the secret thrill of knowing you own what others want. But suppose you were to somehow gain insight into the crux of why people collect art. In that case, you're likely to find a fundamental core of "indescribability," a confounding mass of emotions, impulses, and experiences that causes a collector to fasten on a piece of art like a homing pigeon to its target.

But this is hardly different for the artist than it is for the collector. A prominent artist is quoted to have said, "I found that I could say things with color and shapes that I couldn't say any other way—things I had no words for." Perhaps the artist says, with broad strokes of the brush, words that resonate more deeply with us than we could ever understand, and it is this sense of "the deep calling to the deep" that attracts and holds us more than any tangible reasons we could give for why we collect art.

We know that art is influenced in many ways by the realities and circumstances that surround, and sometimes propel, its creation. If we cannot truly say why we collect, and artists cannot always articulate what they paint, what better way to explore and understand these phenomena than to engage with the works of those who can put these feelings into words with their piercing insight and clarifying thoughts? This review of fictional and nonfictional books, poems, and essays presents the works of Black writers who have engaged with these concepts, and in the pages of these works we may finally come to understand and answer the big questions about Black art and what constitutes the psyche of Black artists.

The review explores these works through six specific genres of Black literature: political/cultural works, fiction, poetry, economics, education, and autobiography/biography.

POLITICAL/CULTURAL WORKS

Black history in the United States may well be one of the longest-running struggles for basic rights, social equity, and true democracy in modern times. The essays reviewed under this genre follow the trend of a compelling narrative that begins a mere forty years after the formal abolition of slavery in the United States and ends with the heartbreaking recognition that the struggle is far from over.

The Souls of Black Folk by W. E. B. Du Bois (1903)

The Souls of Black Folk is a collection of essays by Du Bois tackling everything from music to history to lyrics. Written at the turn of the twentieth century, Du Bois's writings are pivotal because of their place in the historical continuum of race relations in the United States and their critical analysis of events at the time.

The essays are part memoir, part fiction, and part sociological analysis. Written forty years after the end of the American Civil War and the abolition of slavery in the United States, the essays are set against the backdrop of the failed promises of emancipation and the enduring dehumanization of Black people. Du Bois is acutely critical of how the government has failed to handle race matters and of unfair social policies that seem to have replaced *de jure* slavery with political and social subjugation.

The Souls of Black Folk is considered a seminal work of African American history.

Women, Race & Class by Angela Davis (1981)

In a collection of thirteen essays that chart the history of the United States from the slave trade and abolitionist movements to the women's liberation movements, Angela Davis provides both a historical and critical analysis of the role and circumstances of Black women in the United States.

Like the feminist and author bell hooks, Davis's work plays a pivotal role as one of the first discussions of insection of race, gender, and class. Applying Marxist analysis, Davis elucidates the relationship between class, race, and capitalism, and explains how the economic impact of women has been historically neglected from the period of slavery even into the twentieth century. But Davis is also intensely critical of contemporary women's liberation movements, arguing that they have almost exclusively been for and by middle-class White women, often excluding, overlooking, or discriminating against women of color and of different social classes.

Davis argues, as did bell hooks, that these movements were hampered by their leaders' classist and racist tendencies and that they thereby played a role in limiting the progress of women's rights in the United States.

Democracy Matters: Winning the Fight against Imperialism by Cornel West (2004)

Philosopher and political scholar Cornel West rose to national prominence upon the success of his best-selling book *Race Matters*, a deep analysis of the scars, challenges, and casualties of racism in the United States. West follows up his best-seller with *Democracy Matters*, a searing commentary on the challenges to democracy in the modern world and the United States.

West enumerates and describes the fundamental threats to modern democracy in today's world: aggressive militarism, escalating authoritarianism, free-market fundamentalism, and the role that the United States plays in perpetuating these trends. He purports that for United States to succeed in its self-proclaimed role as global "steward of freedom and democracy", the country must first assume responsibility for the deep-rooted systemic injustices and imperialist corruption that continues to plague its democracy and its people.

In mpassioned, analytical, and provocative prose, West makes a case for revitalizing the United States and restoring its democratic tradition through the medium of Socratic questioning, prophetic witnessing, and tragicomic hope.

The Audacity of Hope: Thoughts on Reclaiming the American Dream by Barack Obama (2006)

In terms of political relevance, *The Audacity of Hope* reads like Obama's presidential manifesto. The title of the book is taken from a sermon by Obama's former pastor, Jeremiah Wright, who was, in turn, inspired by a G. F. Watts painting named *Hope*.

The book charts ideas that Obama had first introduced to the world at the Democratic National Convention in 2004 and that eventually formed the basis of many of his policy decisions during his presidency. One observer, former presidential candidate Gary Hart, described the book as Obama's "thesis submission" for the presidency of the United States—and he could not have been more correct.

For those trying to gain a sense of the ideas, core values, and vision that drove Obama during his presidency, *The Audacity of Hope* presents a starting point filled with valuable insight into the enigma that became the forty-fourth president of the United States of America.

Nigger: The Strange Career of a Troublesome Word by Randall Kennedy (2002)

There is hardly a word more deserving of study into its etymology than the focus of Randall Kennedy's short volume. The word *nigger* can connote vitriol, but it can also cement brotherhood. It can be said with irony, pain, or anger, thrown like a grenade, or used to beat someone over the head like the nightstick of an overeager beat cop. But it can also be said with laughter, fun, affection, self-deprecation, or even empowerment.

Harvard Law Professor Kennedy traces the origins, multifarious connotations, and controversies that accompany the use of the word while drawing on a range of references that include Chris Rock punch lines, the Jim Crow South, and Huckleberry Finn. This is definitely worth a read.

How to Be Black by Baratunde Thurston (2012)

Matters of race and racial identity are a complex topic in the United States, especially when stereotypes and interracial relationships are up for discussion. Yet stand-up comedian Baratunde Thurston holds nothing back in this hysterical but biting commentary about being Black (or being anything, for that matter) in the United States.

Through witty commentary interspersed with hilarious autobiographical anecdotes, Thurston introduces Black culture that will "hit the spot" for people acquainted with Black America and bring helpful suggestions for the dilettante amateur on how to appreciate Black people and their culture.

It's not all fun and games, though. Thurston does not shy away from the realities of being Black; instead, he finds a way to present the harsh truth about hurtful stereotypes through his own brand of satire. In his book, Thurston teaches us how to approach issues of race without fear and discomfort.

We Were Eight Years in Power: An American Tragedy by Ta-Nehisi Coates (2017)

We Were Eight Years in Power is a collection of essays written by Ta-Nehisi Coates during each of the eight years of Barack Obama's presidency. The title of the book itself is an allusion to the lament of Reconstruction-era Black political activists who saw the brief sunshine of multiracial democracy in the South unceremoniously eclipsed by a return to White supremacist rule.

The reader will immediately recognize echoes of this tragic history in our own time, especially in light of the unprecedented election of a Black president and the vicious backlash that led to the election of a man Coates describes as America's "first white president." Coates's book provides a bracing account of modern America and the antecedents that have resulted in many wanting to "erase with extreme prejudice" the impressions left from having a Black president.

Ain't I a Woman by Gloria Jean Watkins [bell hooks] (1981)

Black women have always existed at the troubling intersection of race, class, and gender. Yet, this nuance is not often discussed in literature, particularly in feminist literature. Cultural critic Professor Watkins, writing through her pen name "bell hooks," captures these crosshairs powerfully in her book.

The book charts the cultural, economic, and social history of Black women in the United States and the historical oppression they have faced incessantly from White men, Black men, and even White women. Watkins is deeply critical of the feminist movements of the sixties and seventies: led by middle-class White women, these movements failed to appreciate or address the unique challenges that affect Black women.

Ain't I a Woman is particularly poignant, as it presents the fresh perspective of a young female on the cusp of womanhood, emerging into a world in flux and not liking what she sees.

White Girls by Hilton Als (2013)

Acknowledged as "one of the most highly acclaimed essays in years," *White Girls* by Professor Hilton Als confounds as much as it enthralls. This collection of essays is a study in the complex surrealism of otherness, weaving together a brilliant analysis of topics such as art, music, and literature with piercing insight and elegant language.

Als fearlessly discusses polarizing issues such as race, gender, history, identity, and cultural appropriation in a series of essays bursting with unique understanding and wisdom. The first essay, "Tristes Tropiques," has attracted special critical acclaim for the startling rawness of the writing and the remarkable use of language to communicate a plethora of emotions.

Readers who want to challenge themselves to think about cultural issues even deeper will find Als' collection an excellent place to get lost in.

Fiction

Fiction may be make-believe, but the stories that unfold within its pages often portray the realities of life more forcefully than any news story can. These works of fiction approach monumental questions and issues in striking, unforgettable prose. Their stories are layered with the full range of emotions, complications, and intrigue that constitute the true reality of everyday life.

The Man Who Cried I Am by John A. Williams (1925)

The Man Who Cried I Am is a fictional account of the life of a Black journalist named Max Reddick and the struggles he faces in an intensely segregated and racist America.

The book is cinematic as it fades in and out between time periods, mindsets, and settings, all the way from New York to Leiden, from Africa to Amsterdam. Dying of cancer, Reddick travels to Amsterdam to see his estranged wife one last time and also his late friend's mistress, who has a message for him. On the trip,

Reddick reflects on his life. Through his memories, the reader is taken on a journey spanning twenty-four years that tackles everything from the inner workings of the newspaper world to working with President Kennedy. The author includes fictional characters based on real-life personalities such as Malcolm X, James Baldwin, and Richard Wright, situating his novel in a real-world context. The book vividly portrays the realities of living as a Black person in the United States and the challenges of creating enduring change in the circumstances of Black America.

The Bluest Eye by Toni Morrison (1970)

Published in 1970, *The Bluest Eye* is Toni Morrison's first novel. The fictional story is set in Lorain, Ohio, in the years following the Great Depression. It follows the life of Pecola Breedlove, a troubled Black girl who becomes a tragic victim of the mercilessly racist society she lives in.

The story is narrated by Claudia MacTeer, Pecola's foster sister, and from a third-person perspective at certain points. Due to her dark skin and her mannerisms, Pecola is consistently regarded as ugly by many of those around her. Made to feel less than human through her interactions with older White people and her peers, Pecola develops an obsessive fixation on having blue eyes and other traits commonly associated with White people.

Morrison's story poignantly addresses the detrimental effects of racism, body-shaming, and disregard for the emotions of others, as well as the misleading nature of White standards.

Kindred by Octavia E. Butler (1979)

In a slightly unorthodox depiction of slavery in the United States, Butler's novel tells the story of Dana, a modern young Black woman who is suddenly whisked through time away from her apartment in California and into the horrors of the slave-owning Deep South. Butler presents the stark realities of slavery and the complex dynamics of life on a plantation in rich and touching prose.

Dana, having just moved into a new house with her White husband, is celebrating her twenty-sixth birthday when, after feeling dizzy, she abruptly finds herself at the edge of a river surrounded by a forest just in time to save the White son of a slave owner from drowning. She is drawn back through time repeatedly, and she soon learns of her familial ties with the slaves she meets and the dangers that might prevent her from ever seeing her home or husband again.

Although the story seems simple enough, it is undergirded by an intricate interplay of emotions that will keep readers entranced.

The Color Purple by Alice Walker (1982)

The Color Purple is a fictional novel about a group of Black women living in early twentieth-century rural Georgia. The book follows the lives of Celie and her sister Nettie in a heartwarming story of love, redemption, and how people can overcome their struggles to become the best version of themselves. But the story is not one of pure optimism and joy: Walker captures the terrible realities of domestic abuse, sexual abuse, racism, and sexism that Black women of that era were routinely subjected to.

The story is told in the form of letters, first written from Celie to God, and then later to her sister Nettie. We come to know Celie through her letters, to know her huge heart which persists despite the vicious abuse she suffers at the hands of the men in her life. Celie rises above the unfair hand life has dealt her to become her own woman.

The story is written in the stilted, broken grammar of the barely literate Black South at the time. While it's challenging to get into at first, we are soon caught up in the story, and the unique dialect allows the reader to be vividly immersed in the world of our heroine.

Americanah by Chimamanda Ngozi Adichie (2013)

On the surface, *Americanah* is an endearing tale of two young lovers, Ifemelu and Obinze, who experience love, lose it, and then find each other again many years later as accomplished adults. But the deeper story charts the phenomenon and expectations tied to migration from abroad, with the United States serving as a symbol of hope and achievement, and the ultimate disappointment of finding out that the American Dream is a lie.

The story follows the struggle to acclimatize to a new culture through Ifemelu's experience of being an African in the United States and the increasing recognition of her

Blackness amid Whiteness.

Adichie explores multiple themes throughout the book, including the universal questions of race, belonging, and identity in a foreign land. She perfectly captures the identity conflict of Africans in diaspora and the experience of being too African for the West, yet too westernized for Africa. This paradox is referenced in the name of the book, *Americanah*, denoting one who is in a state of limbo, being neither here nor there.

The Hate U Give by Angie Thomas (2017)

The Hate U Give is a young adult fictional novel based on the 2009 police shooting of an unarmed Black man, Oscar Grant. Although the book was eventually released in 2017, it reads like it could have been written in August 2020. The events it describes are strikingly resonant with our times; they read almost like a play-by-play of the deaths of Trayvon Martin, George Floyd, Breonna Taylor, and a host of others who were unceremoniously murdered in a similar fashion.

The story is narrated by sixteen-year-old Alicia Starr, a Black girl from a fictional inner-city neighborhood who witnesses the killing of her childhood friend by a White police officer. The book follows Alicia as she grapples with the weight of what she witnessed and the burden of sharing what she knows with the whole world. Events in the book eventually force her to speak out about the shooting, and she stands up to the police officers who would rather she had kept quiet.

Through the book, Thomas attempts to provide a critical perspective into the pain, disappointment, and fear these shootings cause. If you would like to gain more insight into the motivations of the Black Lives Matter movement, then this is a must-read.

POETRY

These works of poetry approach significant societal issues in beautiful verse and enchanting stanza. They are hard hitting and unapologetic in their treatment of these issues, but they are also delicate and heartwarming, reminding us that even on the darkest of days the sun can still shine through.

For Colored Girls Who Have Considered Suicide/When the Rainbow is Enuf by Ntozake Shange (1975)

For Colored Girls is a series of poems about women of color who face oppression in a racist and sexist society. The impactful stories and experiences narrated through the unique structure of the poems weave a tapestry of hurt, pain, love, loss, and empowerment. The women are not specifically named in any of the poems; rather, each of the seven is identified by only a color.

The book is a series of poetic monologues made into twenty to twenty-two poems. The poems are meant to be accompanied by music and dancing, creating a unique performance known as a choreopoem. Shange also utilizes a unique writing style that includes vernacular and unorthodox punctuation, all meant to increase the auditory experience of the poems.

Shange's work is inspired by events in her life, including her four suicide attempts and her experiences with racism and sexism.

Brown Girl Dreaming by Jacqueline Woodson (2014)

Brown Girl Dreaming is a collection of poems about the birth and youth of the writer herself. Woodson tells the entire story in verse, communicating to young readers her experiences growing up as a Black child in the 1960s, first in Ohio, then in South Carolina, and finally in New York.

As we follow Woodson's journey to maturity, we learn about complex topics like racism, segregation, domestic disharmony, and the bright spots of respect and fairness that remind us that even places tainted by the worst intolerance can hold shining points of light.

Although her coming-of-age story is told against the backdrop of the severe dehumanization of Black people, Woodson chooses to focus her narrative on her love for the places where she grew up, her treasured memories, and her growing awareness of her power to do anything she desires.

ECONOMICS

The only work reviewed here may well have found its way into other genres. However, this would be a disservice to the author and create the risk that its essential economic lessons may be overlooked. If you have wondered at the enigma of Black prosperity and the ideas that may help bring about an economically buoyant Black race, then the work reviewed here is compulsory reading.

PowerNomics: The National Plan to Empower Black America
by Dr. Claud Anderson (2000)

PowerNomics presents, in stark terms, the historical basis and continued operation of the racial monopolies and behavior patterns that demolish the illusion of Black progress. It proposes a framework of solutions, policies, and action steps designed to help construct a Black America that is prosperous and self-sufficient.

While the book was written almost twenty years ago, the circumstances of Black people today clearly show that it remains just as relevant today. The issues it dissects continue to be urgent, and the solutions it proposes are as effective today as they were then. This is a must-read for every Black American looking for new ways to think about and strategize toward achieving Black prosperity.

EDUCATION

While the ivory halls of the most-respected learning institutions in the United States often pride themselves on being sheltered from the complications of political and social issues, the experience of Black people in the United States has shown otherwise. While segregation no longer formally exists in the US educational system today, there are extremely valid arguments that other, equally injurious, experiences have taken its place. These works provide razor-sharp insight into some of these experiences and the effect they have on Black education.

The Privileged Poor: How Elite Colleges Are Failing Disadvantaged Students by Anthony Abraham Jack (2019)

The Privileged Poor explores the factors that contribute to unequal experiences for students of different social and financial backgrounds in elite colleges. Ivy League institutions have done a lot of work to broaden social representation in their student bodies; however, as Jack explains in this book, access is not the same as inclusion.

The book specifically looks at the role that secondary education and college policies play in molding the experiences of two groups of students: the privileged poor and the doubly disadvantaged. Drawing on interviews with undergraduates at one of America's elite schools, as well as his own experiences growing up, Jack describes the disparate effects of college policies on these groups of students and the unequivocal impact that background has on their prospects of success.

A vital nuance that Jack manages to capture through his work is the profound dislocation of the doubly disadvantaged from their original location to their current location at an Ivy League institution. *The Privileged Poor* is an essential read for those who want to understand the intersection between education, race, and class in the United States.

Hooded is a practical guidebook on surviving and thriving in the male-dominated world of STEM as a female doctoral candidate. Malika Grayson presents an honest look at the often unexamined experiences of Black women in higher education.

Higher education environments are often disproportionately male, especially in STEM disciplines. This creates an adverse environment for Black women, who typically have to endure a perpetual uphill battle to earn advanced degrees, facing obstacles ranging from racism and sexism to self-doubt and even classism. Grayson provides practical tips for surviving in this world, drawing on her own experiences as the only Black woman in her Ivy League program. Her account is transparent and honest as she shares her lows and her highs, and the strategies she applied to keep her head above water and ultimately shine in a challenging environment.

AUTOBIOGRAPHY/BIOGRAPHY

This final genre comes last for a reason: it allows us to reflect on the lessons from other genres even as we compare our thoughts, positions, and conclusions with those of the personalities within this genre. A fitting end to an excursion into the psyche of the Black artist and the ideas and beliefs that have potentially shaped the art we now appreciate and collect.

Holler If You Hear Me: Searching for Tupac Shakur
by Michael Eric Dyson (2001)

Having written critically acclaimed texts on the lives of Malcolm X and Martin Luther King Jr., Michael Eric Dyson turns his attention to one of the most enigmatic personalities in African American pop culture: Tupac Shakur. Written just five years after the rapper's murder, Dyson provides unique insight into Shakur's life, death, and the enduring legacy that has brought him to cult status in the eyes of his loyal followers.

A poet, activist, and actor, the twenty-five-year-old rapper was known for his surprisingly introspective music and magnetic personality. Dyson helps us understand why Shakur rose to such fame and how he continues to linger in the hearts of millions around the world. Although one might expect a sympathetic exposé into the life of Shakur, Dyson's account can be as uncomfortably personal as it is sharply analytical.

This work is a must-read for Shakur fans and anyone who wishes to better understand the inner world of the rapper.

Becoming by Michelle Obama (2018)

After breaking records as the first Black First Lady of the United States in 2008, Michelle Obama quickly became a national icon and one of the most compelling women of our time. When many would have expected a staid First Lady, steadfastly living up to the prissy expectations that typically come with the office, she instead showed us a type of First Lady that was original and refreshing, all in a mission to usher in the most inclusive and welcoming White House in recent history.

In her memoir, Obama invites us into her world and gives us an honest, deeply reflective, and at times witty account of the girl that became the woman whom millions of people around the world now love and respect. She describes her lows and highs, both private and public, and the unique sequence of events that helped her become the woman who defies expectations with such grace and poise at every turn.

A Promised Land by Barack Obama (2020)

While *The Audacity of Hope* regales us with a grandiose political vision of a United States fueled by the righteous power of a truly functional democracy, *A Promised Land* tells the story of a "skinny kid with an unusual name" who became America's first Black president.

In this deeply personal account of a history that is now as familiar in the bustling streets of Africa as it is among the high-rises of Europe, Obama manages to provide an intimate and thoughtful perspective of the facts behind history as we now know it. The book takes readers on a journey from the watershed moment at the Iowa caucus victory to the declaration of a Black man as president of the United States and all through the peaks and valleys of Obama's tenure in office.

Obama's account is filled with profound insights into US democracy and an "honest accounting" of his eight years in the Oval Office.

A Most Beautiful Thing is a moving, true account of the formation, experiences, and challenges of America's first all-Black high school rowing team. Arshay Cooper narrates a story of life on the battle-scarred streets of the Westside of Chicago, and living in a neighborhood where the dream of getting out and living clean will remain just that: a dream.

Cooper speaks honestly of his mother's drug addiction, the vicious cycle of drugs and guns in his neighborhood, and watching his friends slowly disappear down the road to criminality on the back of intractable need. He shares how he came to join a newly formed rowing team at school and how this opportunity changed his life, and the lives of his teammates, for good.

On the way to making history on the nation's first Black rowing team, Cooper and his teammates learn teamwork, entrepreneurship, and the realities of competing in an all-White sport. *A Most Beautiful Thing* is a reprint of *Suga Water*, the original story written by the same author in 2015.

Chapter 2

The Power of Visual Albums

Over one hundred years ago, it was said that cinema was the literature of the twentieth century, but Black artists have made visual albums the cinema of the twenty-first century. The progression of art and technology has created the opportunity for visual presentations that add dimension to the music. This chapter examines the incisive message of the film Runaway in light of its symbolism and imagery.

The Love-Hate Relationship between the Artist and the Industry—Kanye West's Film *Runaway (2010)*

So What Is a Visual Album?

A visual album is a tool whereby the artist releases a video to accompany each song on the album. Typically, the videos run together to tell a story in concordance with the lyrics and music. This allows artists to give additional context to the music they produce, leading to more meaningful and multidimensional storytelling and communication than a traditional music video could offer.

The Beatles released one of the first visual albums in 1964: *A Hard Day's Night*. This inspired artists such as The Who, Michael Jackson, Prince, and so many more to follow suit. Although Beyoncé has taken the crown for the most recent and popular visual albums, Prince's *Purple Rain*, Pink Floyd's *The Wall*, Led Zeppelin's *The Song Remains the Same*, and Michael Jackson's *Moonwalker* are just a few iconic visual albums that have helped shaped the genre.

Inspired by Michael Jackson's *Thriller*, Prince's *Purple Rain*, and Pink Floyd's *The Wall*, Kanye West's *Runaway* is an innovative twist on the medium. The almost thirty-five-minute film features ten songs from the album *My Beautiful Dark Twisted Fantasy*, which had not even been released yet. Featuring everything from marching bands to fireballs, fireworks, and ballerinas, it is a genuinely extravagant production.

Let us delve into some of the symbols and themes that make up the visual experience of Kanye West's film *Runaway*, set to the songs and music of *My Beautiful Dark Twisted Fantasy*. What does the imagery tell us about Kanye's inspiration and struggles, and about the relationship between the artist and the music industry?

REBIRTH OF THE PHOENIX

The phoenix is a Greek mythological creature. When it dies, it takes power from the last bird so that it can be reborn. This is representative of the sentiment "living and learning."

This cycle of death and rebirth directly parallels Kanye's career as a creative, wavering between praise and crucifixion from the media for years. Throughout his tumultuous career, he has become a polarizing figure, as he is not afraid to speak his mind regardless of the repercussions. Much like the phoenix, Kanye's creative career consists of learning from his mistakes and evolving into an evolved, more refined artist.

West has even stated, "It definitely relates to everything that I've been through, like, burning to the ashes and rebuilding and becoming a better person and delivering a better product."

"DARK FANTASY"

The film begins with the striking image of West playing the character Griffin, who is running from something unknown and ominous. The lighting is harsh as we see a luminescent red fog seemingly catching up with and enveloping him.

We hear Mozart's "Lacrimosa Dies Illa," which translates to "full of tears will be that day." This last part of the third section of Mozart's *Requiem* mass is based on the Latin sequence "Dies Irae," meaning "the day of wrath." The song ends with the speaker pleading for redemption, a sentiment that is all too familiar for Kanye. In a way, it speaks of his life in the spotlight up until his *My Beautiful Dark Twisted Fantasy* era. Does this signify Kanye running away from judgment day?

The scene quickly transitions to a meteorite barreling toward the forest as the camera pulls back into outer space. All the stars remain visible while the clouds move rapidly. Kanye is seen driving a Murciélago that he soon crashes when the meteorite touches down.

We see Griffin get out of the car and stand over the phoenix momentarily rather than save her. The aerial camera shot showcases Kanye's first glance at the phoenix and her delicately colored feathers. This could be illustrative of Kanye's creativity and innocence—beautiful and delicate.

Griffin then carries her back to his home, where we notice a news anchor reporting on the mysterious fires causing major destruction. Griffin interrupts, saying, "First rule in this world, baby—don't pay attention to anything you see in the news." Kanye's statement directly applies to his personal life, with the media constantly berating, criticizing, and using him for headlines. Regardless of the accuracy, Kanye is often depicted as the villain.

"GORGEOUS"

The phoenix starts walking around the backyard, a safe, controlled space. She is inquisitive about the new environment around her, touching the grass, the leaves, and even getting close to some of the innocent animals. This scene is a kind of metaphor for Kanye's early career: as a new artist, he was free to explore many different facets of music without the scrutiny of the outside world or the media.

The scene ends abruptly by mimicking Kanye's catapult to fame through the mainstream media.

"Power (Remix)"

In a compelling scene, we see Kanye use a touchpad to play the weakened phoenix "Power (Remix)." She is pictured on the couch, struggling to move after the violent crash. Still, he slowly imbues her with power through the music, and we see her strengthen and beginn to rebuild her muscles through dance. This scene is symbolic of the power of music, whether you're a regular person—or Kanye West. At his lowest moments, music and creativity become a source of inspiration, helping restore him in his personal life and his career. It is the ultimate source of his power.

"All of the Lights"

A young boy, perhaps a stand-in for Kanye's inner child, leads the celebration of joy and life through music. Music is one of the most potent forces on the planet; it can inspire, motivate, captivate, and express our inner demons. Although the young boy is surrounded by darkness, he allows the light, or the music, to lead him through with confidence.

We then notice Griffin (Kanye) showing the phoenix an extravagant fireworks display representative of fame. The phoenix is engrossed in the display, but Griffin gazes at her instead, caring more about her reaction and already numb to the accolades of fame.

Later on, we see a float adorned with Michael Jackson's head. Kanye has expressed his admiration for the King of Pop on multiple occasions, even citing him as an inspiration for the album and film. We notice an angel on the float next to Michael, but despite the extravagance of the moment, there is a darkness surrounding the celebration that the phoenix is oblivious to.

Enter some masked men reminiscent of the Ku Klux Klan. As the scene continues, the young boy dons a mask while still holding the torch. This is a reference to the hold the music industry has over naïve artists looking to create music, the way the industry steals the innocence of artists and exploits their immaturity for gain, leaving them a shell of their former selves.

"DEVIL IN A NEW DRESS"

Griffin and Phoenix enter an all-white themed dinner party reminiscent of the Last Supper. All the guests are dressed in their most lavish white clothing, while Kanye wears a pink suit with black lapels. Phoenix is resplendent in her multihued feathers. We see the guests staring incredulously as they walk to their seats upon realizing that Phoenix is a bird. Interestingly, the guests at the table are all African immigrants in suits eating and drinking without platters or silverware while White servants wait on them. Kanye here shines a light on the disparities in Black wealth: although they may have a seat at the table, they still do not have the platters or utensils, signifying that they don't truly belong.

As everyone begins to eat, Griffin is interrupted by another guest who says, "Your girlfriend is really beautiful ... Do you know she's a bird?"

GRIFFIN SAYS, "I NEVER NOTICED THAT!"

The guest responds, "I mean, like, leave the monkey in the zoo."

At this point, Griffin is confronted with the plain truth: his girlfriend doesn't belong in his circle. He knows that fame strips away any individuality, creativity, character, and morality a person may have, but rather than defend his girlfriend or simply leave the company, he goes on to play the title track, "Runaway."

"RUNAWAY"

Griffin plays on a white piano while ballerinas in all-black costumes perform. Even though the music is beautiful, it's worth noting that the ballerinas remain enshrouded in the same darkness from previous scenes.

The song is riddled with the torment of loving someone while knowing that you're not good for them. As Griffin plays, Phoenix becomes enamored with him, for music is her light. Although Griffin knows that his world will hurt Phoenix, he refuses to break decorum for her.

"Hell of a Life"

A turning point is reached when the main course is served. Horror of horrors! A bird similar to Phoenix is presented on a platter for the guests to eat. Aghast at the sight, she unfolds her wings, screaming and causing the guests to flee. The bird on the table is a sacrifice for the greed of the entertainment industry; they will feast on creatives until the talents lose their individuality and begin to conform to industry standards. This is a cycle Kanye has struggled with throughout his career.

"Blame Game"

Phoenix resides in Griffin's backyard once more, in the safe, controlled space she once found so comforting. This time, she looks defeated and uninterested in the animals and her surroundings. She then turns to Griffin: "All of the statues that we see . . . Where do you think they came from?"

He begins to say, "I think that artists carved them years and years ago—"

She interrupts with, "No! They are phoenixes turned to stone." As Griffin chuckles, she goes on to say, "Do you know what I hate most about your world? Anything that is different, you try to change. You try to tear it down. You rip the wings off the phoenix, and they turn to stone. And if I don't burn, I will turn to stone. If I don't burn, I can't go back to my world."

Griffin doesn't want Phoenix to burn and return to her

world; he says that he will never let her burn. This speaks volumes about the world of fame that Kanye has found himself trapped in. Fame requires you to be stripped of your freedom and individuality in exchange for renown and a staged appearance. The statue represents the loss of individuality as a person is stripped of their character, torn down, and "turned to stone."

Kanye has already become a statue, and he has been one for so long that he can't imagine being free like Phoenix. But to burn is to be born again and to be free.

"Lost in the World"

Griffin wakes up to find that Phoenix is gone while "Lost in the World" plays in the background. He immediately knows where she has gone. The story comes full circle as we see him running through the woods in an echo of the scene that the film opened with. The audience now realizes that he was actually running *toward* rather than away from something in the beginning. He tries to catch Phoenix, but she is already flying away. All he can do is watch.

"Who Will Survive in America?"

The final song in the film and on the album *My Beautiful Twisted Dark Fantasy*—"Who Will Survive in America"— is a condensed version of Gil-Scott Heron's "Comment #1," a poem that paints a vision of the alliance between the White left and the radical Black. This represents the prospects for Kanye in the music industry. It perfectly summarizes the entire film: Is decadence and fame worth it? What do we lose in the process of gaining fame? And does any of it matter in the end?

Both *Runaway* and *My Beautiful Dark Twisted Fantasy* mark an introspective landmark in Kanye's career. The film's message is one that still resonates with listeners today, maybe now more than ever. Its exploration of instability and pressure in the world of celebrities is only amplified by Kanye's more recent work, *The Life of Pablo*, which discusses a range of topics, including mental health, the effects of the media, and the pressures of fame.

True, *Runaway* has elevated Kanye to a level many could only dream of reaching, but the fundamental question remains: is it all worth it? When artists reach the status of an icon like Kanye, they are often perceived as being indestructible. We can see that this isn't the case: Kanye struggles with his mental health issues just like many of us.

And so, the album's message is maintains relevance today: after achieving fame, wealth, and excess, how much of a person's character stays intact, and how much of it turns to stone?

Album Cover: *My Beautiful Dark Twisted Fantasy* by Kanye West

Apart from being Kanye West's fifth album, *My Beautiful Dark Twisted Fantasy* is also the rapper's most critically acclaimed work. The album followed a period of great personal controversy for the rapper and constitutes something of a rebirth with a symbolic rising from the ashes. The album has gained international recognition and was named the Best Rap Album at the 2012 Grammy Awards, alongside being awarded several other honors.

Kanye's music is not the only remarkable thing about the album. I mentioned in *The Black Market* that from "his collaboration with Virgil Abloh and KAWS on his album *808's* to *My Beautiful Dark Twisted Fantasy's* George Condo cover, he continues to commission artists to bring his ideas to life." George Condo's album cover artwork has received as much critical acclaim as the songs in the album. The artwork depicts two nude figures. The male is straddled by an armless female with wings—a phoenix, in keeping with Kanye's symbolic rebirth and renewal through the cathartic release of his music.

The album cover was named one of the fifty greatest album covers of all time by MusicRadar, named by Billboard as the thirtieth best of all time, and listed by NME as the seventh best of the twenty-first century, so far.

Chapter 3

Can Art Retell History?

The two topics covered in this chapter explore the artist's license in modifying art to reinterpret or reinforce cultural values of the past.

TITUS KAPHAR—SHIFTING THE GAZE

"Why do they have to walk?"

This was the question Titus Kaphar's nine-year-old son asked as they walked through the doors of the National Museum of Natural History in Washington, DC. Confronted with the majestic sculpture of Theodore Roosevelt, depicting the historical figure astride his powerful horse and flanked by an African American and a Native American on foot, the little boy asked the question most of us fail to consider or express: "Why?"

Kaphar says the question stopped him in his tracks. This started a process of rumination that would culminate in his 2017 TED talk titled "Can Art Amend History?" and his painting *Shifting the Gaze*.

So much of history as we know it, including art history, is colored by a Western (or European) bias that elevates its own to the devaluation of other communities and cultures. This presents a skewed version of events that focuses our gaze elsewhere and prevents a complete understanding of our past. Kaphar advocates for the importance of telling, in both written and visual mediums, the stories of historically marginalized groups.

His painting and TED talk emphasize that it is time to dissect, reconsider, and expand our historical narratives to present a more honest and inclusive history.

ART IS A LANGUAGE

Shifting the Gaze is a replica of a painting by seventeenth-century Dutch painter Franz Hals. Hals's classic painting, titled *Family Group in a Landscape*, is a portrait of a wealthy family attired in rich silk, lace, brocade, and fine, soft leather boots. The father stands tall in the painting and is flanked by his wife and son, with his beautiful daughter off to the side. The portrait is set against a backdrop of fertile, lush forest and, in the distance, a partially obscured landscape.

The painting includes one more figure: a young Black boy, most likely the house servant. He is set a little behind the family and between the two women. His face is barely discernible, and only a part of his body is visible, the rest lost in the shadows.

As Kaphar argues, Franz Hals's painting tells an incomplete story. Hals includes plenty of detail to inform us of the family's circumstances, story, and wealth. But Hals offers precious little about the story of the boy. This is what Kaphar does differently: rather than leaving the Black boy melded into the background foliage, Kaphar makes the boy the center of attraction. The boy's carefully rendered, illuminated face draws the viewer's eye instantly and naturally. Then, Kaphar obscures the other figures behind broad strokes of white paint, leaving only the boy visible amidst a barrage of white paint.

According to Kaphar, painting is a language. In many ways, it forms the words with which history is written. Whether intentionally or not, the artists' works can and do become part of history, and what the artist chooses to reveal or obscure through their painting becomes a part of the historical narrative. Although so much of Western art contains artwork that reveals a painfully racist, imperialist, and classist history, Kaphar makes the case that it is possible to correct the narrative. Kaphar's body of work shows that art can be a tool for this correction, that it is possible to refocus the spotlight on the neglected corners of our history. He answers the question in his TED talk: yes, art can amend history. But it does that "not by getting rid of stuff," but by shifting the gaze.

To underline this truth, Kaphar notes that the white paint he used on his painting will not permanently erase the figures. It contains linseed oil mixed into the white oil paint, and this will become transparent with age, allowing the obscured figures to reemerge slowly. But in the interim, the white paint will have done its job: forcing us to look with new understanding at the figure, story, and significance of the little Black boy.

Kaphar also makes a case through his painting for changing how we appreciate art, both classical and contemporary. He invites us to look at art in a new light, one that respects and understands the true state of history. For just as history has been unfair to marginalized groups, many classical and contemporary thoughts we have about art were formed alongside or as a result of this incomplete narrative. By shifting our gaze, we can expand our understanding of art, history, and the complex nature of the records his work documents.

COLLECTING WITH A BALANCED UNDERSTANDING

Art collecting can also fall victim to many of the occluding influences that alter art history and art. This is why a better understanding of art history may be critical to truly understanding and enjoying art. With the correct contextual information, a simple drawing of a family in the fields can take on amplified significance and unveil profound truths lurking just beneath the thin veneer of oil paint.

It is almost impossible to properly appreciate art without knowing its history, the stories surrounding it, and the complex nuances of the art itself. Audrey Adams in *The Black Market* said, "My primary mission is to form a collection that reflects history and also that I can pass on to my heirs." This is where the value and joy of collecting lies. With a proper understanding of art history and its complexity, we can better revel in artists like Kaphar who reference art history in their contemporary works.

And just as the artist could shift the gaze to ennoble the Black slave, we now turn our eyes to depictions of violence from two different places and times: those of Picasso and those of contemporary Harlem artist Faith Ringgold.

GUERNICA AND DIE—DIFFERENT TIME FRAMES, SAME ABUSE

In these polarizing times, critics return again and again to *Guernica* (1937), Pablo Picasso's large-scale painting on view at the Museo Reina Sofia in Madrid. The work is a statement against war, depicting the brutality innocent people face when confronted with political upheaval. Another work well worth revisiting during this period of racial tension and general unrest is a warm-hued, vibrant piece completed in 1967 by Faith Ringgold titled *American People Series #20 Die*. Similar in structure to Picasso's renowned canvas, Ringgold imbues her immersive piece with color and racially infused storytelling—but we'll get to that later when we compare and contrast the two paintings. No doubt there's a great deal to learn from such artists and Picasso and Ringgold as we navigate the tumult of 2020.

SPANISH CIVIL WAR 1937

Let's first approach the complex analysis of Picasso's *Guernica*. In 1937, Picasso completed what many consider to be his most striking political masterpiece.

At 11x26 feet, the massive oil on canvas work unveils a polarizing scene, foreshadowing the forthcoming Second World War while revealing the horrors of the ongoing Spanish Civil War. The artist's motivation in creating the work was to shed light on the German bombing of the Basque town Guernica—the piece's namesake, which the artist had seen featured in several newspaper articles. While Picasso painted the commission from the comfort of his Parisian home, the work was ultimately exhibited at the Spanish display of the 1937 Paris International Exposition and later at other global venues.

The touring exhibition showcasing *Guernica* helped bring political attention to the Spanish Civil War, and it became widely recognized in fundraising efforts. Picasso began preliminary work on the piece in January 1937, before even having a clear subject in mind, sketching the beginnings of the chaotic scene—subdued colors; bodies with expressions skewed, positioned in all directions; other motifs we'll explore shortly—before honing in on his precise subject in April of that same year.

Yet, rather than offering a detailed take on the bombing itself, the lauded canvas is something of a statement piece, a generic protest against the atrocities of war. Picasso invites viewers to gaze upon the tragic scene and immerse themselves in the devastation of society, the destruction with which even the most innocent civilians must grapple.

The work is epic, and the lack of color journalistic in nature—not unlike a surrealist photograph. And, while some critics are weary of the work's political motif, no doubt the artist deliberately incorporated the theme of destruction into his piece. Some interpret the looming bull or Minotaur in view on the canvas's left-hand side as representative of the artist's ego, while others claim it evokes the perils of fascism. In either case, it's dominating, emblematic of heightened power and corruption overtaking the scene. Picasso himself has expressed that it represents brutality and darkness, while the screaming horse near the work's center depicts the people of Guernica. Meanwhile, the subtle crying harlequin delves deep into themes of duality, examining the contrast of life and death amid the gray tonality.

Art historian and *Guernica* scholar Anthony Blunt asserts that the animals and human beings may well come together for different reasons: the animals—a muscled bull, winged bird, and injured horse—embody the physicality of war. On the other hand, the human beings offer a more emotional take on the situation: the dead soldier, a woman peering out the window, a devastated mother holding her dead infant, another female subject wailing with arms outstretched as a building burns. In the last eighty-some years, the canvas has become a chilling reminder of the perils of warfare. The stunning irony, many have come to note, is that the scene's chaos is now, in fact, a symbol of peace—a warning sign.

THE CIVIL RIGHTS MOVEMENT OF THE 1960s

This brings us to Ringgold's equally polarizing work. The Harlem-born painter set out to document cultural identity in the United States in the 1960s. While the

Black contemporary artist focused on an entirely different setting than Picasso, her works feature several parallels. In particular, Ringgold's *American People Series #20 Die* sheds light on race relations in the 1960s. I wrote in *The Black Market* that "she wanted her masterpiece to show people that the riots were not just 'poor people breaking into stores' but that they were, rather, about 'people trying to maintain their position, and people trying to get away.'" The 6x12 foot oil on canvas work is a colorful mural-sized interpretation of racial violence. Showcasing the riots overtaking the country at the time, Ringgold's 1967 diptych features an interracial group of men, women, and children, spattered with blood and wearing fearful expressions—a ghastly indication that all are involved and weary of the carnage. The subjects are wearing tailored dresses and business attire, revealing that even the most affluent must be held accountable for the violence that accompanied the Civil Rights movement.

Yet *Die* visibly pays homage to *Guernica* with its scale and abstraction, though Ringgold's canvas depicts an entirely different era. And where the children in Picasso's work exist in large part as emblems of the past—symbols of their parents' fear—Ringgold's youth take a more central role in *Die*, with a pair of terrified children holding each other tightly near the center of the painting, starkly conveying their fear of the future. The Black girl and the White boy cower, terrified yet unified, perhaps a reminder of the notion that prejudice is societal rather than innate. "Children have to be taught that some other people who don't look like them are not right," Ringgold has said, reinforcing the deliberate nature of contrasting such innocence alongside the barbarism of the adults in her work.

The scene is a rich red-yellow bloodbath, a mass of bodies much like those depicted in *Guernica*; indeed, the race riots were still ongoing when Ringgold completed the work. The twentieth piece in her series is the only one in which she references the riots directly—the blood, the death, and the chaotic frenzy that took place amid the turmoil. While Picasso focuses on the aftermath of a bombing, Ringgold takes a more dynamic approach in the violence depicted, with her figures suspended mid-act; again, it's difficult to tell who is instigating the brutality and who is merely on the receiving end. (One can assume that both sides are culpable, just as everyone involved must also face the consequences of their actions.)

In *Die*, Black and White people hold one another, stab one another, and cry to one another. Both men and women, Black and White, bear weapons, hurt one another using their own hands, and console one another thereafter, creating a genuinely engulfing rebellion— an entanglement with the times, with the viewer, and among Ringgold's subjects. It begs the question: who is responsible for the unrest? And what can be done to solve the underlying problems behind it?

INNOCENT BYSTANDERS AS ALWAYS

Die was based on the political movement of the 1960s, yet these same questions hold true today. Where Picasso memorializes the violence of the Spanish Civil

War, Ringgold documents the frenzied brutality of the American race riots of the 1960s. She seeks to abstract the fights, revealing that they involved both race and class, and that all were implicated in the violence. Remarkably, the work delves deep into the ambiguity of what one might do to build a more equitable future, speaking to viewers from all backgrounds in a statement of colorful and fluid iconography, a warning of what must be done before society can heal. It is primarily a warning against social unrest, a cautionary tale of what might occur in the case of collective ignorance, and the artist's take on the unsettling power of seemingly clean-cut protagonists.

Both Picasso and Ringgold, in their respective pieces, convey the brutal message that ignorance is not bliss and that tension must be addressed before additional bystanders get hurt. The two produced canvases have been exceptionally received by critics, with *Die* evoking the moving power of abstract Black contemporary art well before its time, setting the tone for the future.

Just as Picasso inspired Ringgold, perhaps Ringgold will rouse 2020 artists to offer their responses to *Guernica*, helping in their own ways to build a more inclusive, racially equitable future.

In the next chapter, you will find more on Titus Kaphar, together with a fascinating juxtaposition of European neoclassicism and Black contemporary art featured in the Brooklyn Museum.

Chapter 4

Why Encyclopedic Muse-ums Matter

This analysis of encyclopedic museums highlights the importance of art history and the growing interest in Black contemporary art. It examines the Brooklyn Museum in particular, an institution deeply committed to showcasing the works of pioneers who are reshaping what it means to be Black in the United States. This is the place for viewers, curators, and academics to deepen their understanding of what it means to reinterpret art and breach traditional bounds in the space.

A QUEST TO RESHAPE ART: THE BROOKLYN MUSEUM

What Are Encyclopedic Museums?

With a sea of information about art at our disposal, what is the best approach to grounding ourselves in the history of art in a meaningful way? How can we properly/accurately classify art? Can we do so organizationally, by color, by time period, by continent or societal group?

Encyclopedic museums—also known as "universal" museums—are an ideal place to start. These institutions offer visitors information on a full range of subjects, providing a comprehensive overview of art history by featuring a regional-to-global approach to the storied pieces on display.

According to James Cuno, president and director of the Art Institute of Chicago, encyclopedic museums "play an especially important role in the building of civil society" and "encourage curiosity about the world." These institutions are indispensable when 3.4 percent of the global population reside outside their country of birth. There's constant movement in our society, and by studying unlikely artistic connections, both art history and encyclopedic museums can continue to foster a shared sense of human history and contextualized narratives.

Classification, organization, and understanding are just some of the boons encyclopedic museums offer. Today, art historians have come to understand the significance of these encyclopedic museums' diverse collections. They help prevent us from losing sight of our history and cultural understanding—which brings us to the true power of art history. We'll discuss this by focusing on the Brooklyn Museum, a quintessential center for art that embodies all that it means to be a universal, encyclopedic institution, complete with examples from different regions and periods. With contemporary masters hearkening back to their old-master counterparts, the Museum's curators reveal how important it is to garner an accurate, thorough, and ultimately critical understanding of art history.

Why Does Art History Matter?

To be blunt, art history matters in that it allows us to classify how we understand cultures, periods, and genres. It provides vital information on the transition from one sociopolitical stage to another, allowing viewers to glean knowledge from their studies, formulate their own artistic opinions, and draw connections. While art history majors accounted for less than 0.2 percent of the workforce in 2011, this tiny group plays a critical role in the way we curate and view art. The discipline features a unique blend of economics, politics, sociology, and anthropology, investigating a plethora of media, cultures, and messaging that allow the general public to draw conclusions and evaluate different artworks and epochs.

Art history matters because it offers an immersive perspective on world cultures, traditions, and milestones—not only by shedding light on specific events but also by ensuring we take the time needed to interpret encrypted messages for the general public. Art history reveals clues to the way we lived in the past, to the symbols, colors, and materials specific cultures used during various times. Everything from gender roles to wealth distribution to societal values becomes apparent through the eyes of an art historian, as we will soon see in the Brooklyn Museum case study.

For the time being, we will focus on the way that art history allows viewers, trained historians, and the public at large to decode symbolism, deduce what mattered to a group of people at a given time, and understand how these individuals might have wanted to be remembered.

In turn, comparing works through the lens of art history in tandem with a more objective take on events and people provides a well-rounded perspective, thus allowing us to make empowered decisions both in society at large and the artistic community. Encyclopedic museums are a catalyst for achieving just that.

Encyclopedic Museums in the United States: The Brooklyn Museum Case Study

In the United States, the New York Metropolitan Museum of Art in New York, the Detroit Institute of Arts, the Boston Museum of Fine Arts, the Chicago Institute of Art, the Los Angeles County Museum of Art, the Washington D.C. Smithsonian American Art Museum, the Philadelphia Museum of Art, and the Houston Museum of Fine Arts all offer a unique glimpse into the global populations that have helped to shape society, our values, our world, and our shared and individual artistry.

The Brooklyn Museum is yet another acclaimed universal institution. It offers a comprehensive, immersive curatorial experience with powerful insights into contemporary Black art and the pieces, genres, and figures who inspired it. Those who are exclusively focused on art by Black artists *must* include resources and experiences offered by the Brooklyn Museum to enhance their understanding of the genre and deepen the impact of the art they study. The institution, art historians will find, is deeply committed to showcasing the works of pioneers who are reshaping what it means to be Black in the United States and who themselves have studied art history so they can pave the way for a better future.

Let's begin by examining a series of recent exhibitions.

Among them is *KAWS: Along the Way* that took place from June 10, 2015, through March 27, 2016. KAWS is an internationally acclaimed, New Jersey–born, and Brooklyn-based artist who bridges the gap between traditional art and pop culture (by way of references to TV shows like *The Simpsons, SpongeBob SquarePants*, and others) in his vibrant paintings and large-scale sculptures. His eighteen-foot wood sculpture *Along the Way* (2013) features two oversized emotional figures that reinforce the secret feelings of popular cartoon characters. Decorating the museum lobby during the exhibition, the work reflected the multifaceted nature of our most beloved characters while highlighting the contrast between their commercialization and cultural significance.

By aligning the artist with the colorful, fluid paintings of Nina Chanel Abney and Mickalene Thomas's commoditized pieces adorned with rhinestone and acrylics, the Brooklyn Museum leverages KAWS to honor the narratives that have shaped the artistic trajectories and values of young Black talent. Symbolism, a free exchange of ideas around commercialization, and an abundant use of color come together to culminate in a clear understanding of the exhaustive nature of Black art in America today.

In addition, the *Infinite Blue* exhibition, held at the Brooklyn Museum from November 25, 2016 through November 5, 2018, laid the foundation for a more thorough understanding of the blue theme in art from ancient Egypt through the present. The exhibition featured a curated cross-generational, global, and multidisciplinary selection of works that examined the use of the color blue as a symbol of beauty, power, and spirituality. Gender roles, gender differences, and modern feminist thinking came into play during this universal take on art featuring the color blue.

For this multinational and multicultural exhibition, the Brooklyn Museum pulled from its Asian, Egyptian, African, American, Native American, and even European collections, combining paintings, drawings, prints, and sculptures to achieve a well-classified curation of the color blue depicted in art. Ceramic masterpieces from Asia, European manuscripts, images of South Asian deities, and paintings showcasing the color blue in nature were prevalent. *Wine Jar with Fish and Aquatic Plants* (n.d.), an early example of Chinese blue-and-white porcelain, and more contemporary works like American artist Joseph Kosuth's *276 On Color Blue* (1990) reinforced how art historians might organize and classify works from different locations and periods to touch on common themes.

It's worth noting that blue in color theory is considered a color of maturity: an adult color in pornographic blue movies; a metaphor for sadness, as human beings frequently describe the state of being "blue"; and a strong reference to the natural world. If you look at our planet from space, you'll see that the Earth is 75 percent blue—the color of the ocean. Contemporary artists such as Yves Klein and Gregory Coates reference this in the blue pigments that embellish their paintings, offering a contemporized perspective of art history once again exquisitely curated by the Brooklyn Museum.

Moving on to an exhibition held from January 26

to March 11 of that same year, *One Basquiat* depicts the work of Jean-Michel Basquiat, a Brooklyn-born artist of Haitian and Puerto Rican descent. Basquiat's work is integral to Black contemporary art within the borough and across the globe. In 1980, the artist embarked on a transition from a street artist writing aphorisms on the walls and streets of Brooklyn to an internationally renowned gallery artist. The Brooklyn Museum expertly contextualized this journey by placing a single painting on display: the 1982 painting *Untitled*, a gripping, colorful abstract portrait of a disembodied head.

Emblematic of Basquiat's early success and fast-tracked rise through the New York art space cut short by his premature death, the exhibition, through the generosity of Tokyo collector Yusaku Maezawa, is further proof of how all parties involved in the curatorial process can help to contextualize art. In reference to his acquisition of *Untitled*, Maezawa stated, "When I first encountered this painting, I was struck with so much excitement and gratitude for my love of art ... I hope it brings as much joy to others as it does to me, and that this masterpiece by the twenty-one-year-old Basquiat inspires our future generations."

The retrospective, in turn, highlighted the Brooklyn Museum's commitment to the artist's dynamic personal story, reinforcing its commitment to how Basquiat might inspire future artists and art historians.

It may sound counterintuitive, but those faithfully entrenched in the art world—talent, curators, collectors, and committed viewers—accept that we cannot fully appreciate contemporary Black art without paying homage to European artists like Pablo Picasso, Francisco Goya, Vincent van Gogh, and other disruptors. This brings us to *Rembrandt to Picasso: Five Centuries of European Works on Paper*, held at the Brooklyn Museum from June 21 through October 13, 2019.

The exhibition revealed how artists have worked on paper to depict worlds both real and imagined, experimenting with materials and techniques to communicate their personal and political views. Pastels, pencil sketches, etchings, and so many more mediums were used. The idea behind this exhibition was to offer an intimate insight into the artist's dexterous hand. Four chronological sections move from the early sixteenth century through the early twentieth century, honing in on over one hundred European works on paper straight from the Brooklyn Museum's collection.

Multidisciplinary in nature, the works of James Tissot, Berthe Morisot, Suzanne Valadon, and many others honor the Western canon *and* pay homage to women artists and artists of color, exploring each individual's artistic practice in line with the broader visual landscape of the era. Portraiture, landscape, and satire alongside studies, finished pieces, and other études across genres come together to reveal the cultural conditions under which European art blossomed over time.

The exhibition also prompted key questions about whether an artist's work can be assessed separately from their beliefs and from the cultural period in which they worked. Moreover, it revealed how European artists were influenced by their travels to Africa and the South Pacific, from Paul Gauguin's *Tahitian Woman* (1894) to Emil Nolde's *South Sea* (1915) along with Picasso's *Nude Standing in Profile* (1906), which drew from ancient Iberian art. Held appropriately in tandem with the adjacent *One: Titus Kaphar* exhibition, *Rembrandt to Picasso: Five Centuries of European Works on Paper* reminds us how artists, through their personal experiences, might evolve in their use of tools and materials, experiment with new genres and compositions, and find inspiration in seemingly unlikely places.

Finally, we explore *Jacques-Louis David Meets Kehinde Wiley,* an exhibition from January 24 through March 12, 2020. Kehinde Wiley—a legendary New York–based painter known for his vibrant, naturalistic portraits of Black people—and French neoclassical pioneer Jacques-Louis David come together in this unprecedented exhibition. The Brooklyn Museum showcased Wiley's triumphant *Napoleon Leading the Army over the Alps* (2005) alongside the nineteenth-century canvas that inspired it: David's *Bonaparte Crossing the Alps* (1800–01). The pairing of these portraits created more than two centuries apart yet touching on a common theme offers an in-depth commentary on race, power, masculinity, and how historians craft a common narrative.

Both artists have been pivotal in documenting history in real time. David was commissioned by Napoleon himself, helping to redefine painting in Europe, while Wiley's *Napoleon Leading the Army over the Alps* depicts an unidentified Black man in captivating modern streetwear riding horseback in frame, a patterned red curtain serving as the backdrop for this twist on heroic victory and equestrian art. Each artist sets the stage in his own way—and by way of the Brooklyn Museum and the Musée national des châteaux de Malmaison et Bois-Préau's curatorial genius—for political commentary, social change, and contemporary artistic trends in their respective eras. The result is an inarguable link between French Neoclassicism and Black contemporary art; a rewrite of art history, if you will.

As mentioned previously, from June 21 through October 13, 2019, the Brooklyn Museum held the exhibit *One: Titus Kaphar* to great acclaim. Kaphar, whose work rewrites art history by showcasing Black subjects at the forefront of his canvases, whitewashed his painting *Shifting the Gaze* (2017), based on *Family Group in a Landscape* (1648) by renowned Dutch painter Frans Hals. This single-piece exhibition obscures parts of the group portrait with erratically but intentionally placed white paint, drawing attention to a young Black boy who had been relegated to the margins of the canvas (and thus to the margins of European society) in Hals's seventeenth-century work. To tell the stories of those traditionally excluded, Kaphar hones in on the European bias through which history—art history included—is often written, advocating for a more inclusive narrative.

BREACHING TRADITIONAL BOUNDS

On display at major encyclopedic museums, works spanning time periods are internationally celebrated and studied extensively by academics to better understand how cultures have evolved. For one, the sculptures of ancient Greece and Renaissance Italy quickly spread throughout Europe and the Americas. By sharing these collections, viewers and artists were able to comingle and make powerful statements on their respective societies' impacts on their contemporary worlds. After being observed, studied, and shared, these works went on to inspire other civilizations' art. And the works showcased at the Brooklyn Museum—outlined above across numerous exhibitions—are no exception, particularly where Black contemporary art is concerned.

Chapter 5

The Emergence of Public Art

As an art form that transcends the boundaries of traditional art, public artworks have overcome many of the obstacles and criticisms that the art world faces. In this chapter, we'll take a look at the bold initiatives of three artists who use their public space creations to counter conventions and stereotypes.

The most common perception of art is that it is a pastime reserved for the privileged few. I stated in *The Black Market*, "When entering an art gallery, it's likely that you'll notice white walls, white cube designs, and quiet spaces. This is purely a marketing tactic many galleries use to convey an air of affluence. These establishments are designed to attract elite, educated, and sophisticated individuals and institutions. This façade creates a psychological barrier that discourages people who do not fall in the 'elitist' category from attending gallery showings. And ultimately, from collecting the art." In contrast, public artworks reach beyond the elitist sphere, as they are placed in the public space—not in a gallery, museum, or private collection—for everybody to see, touch, and enjoy.

Public buildings have inspired some artists to cultivate unique new media to showcase art to the public, as we can see from the architectural transformations of Theaster Gates.

Historically, one of the most common art forms within the public art sphere has been sculpture. By Western conventions, sculptures have been confined almost exclusively to White men as a way of celebrating their influence on society, to the exclusion of people of color. However, artists such as Kehinde Wiley and Simone Leigh have subverted the inherent biases of these presentations by introducing Black figures into an art medium that has hitherto excluded them.

THEASTER GATES—REJUVENATING STRUCTURES THROUGH ART

Theaster Gates was responsible for the conceptual design and presentation of a major arts event in the UK called *Sanctum,* produced by the Brighton arts organization Situations as part of Bristol 2015 European Green Capital. The event involved creating a temporary structure within the shell of the fourteenth-century Temple Church in Bristol, which was bombed and mostly destroyed during the Second World War. As a part of the performance, Gates curated a 552-hour show aimed at producing a continuous sea of sound for twenty-four days and twenty-four nights by over a thousand different artists.

The *Sanctum* website describes the range of such artistic renditions from drag to hymns, poetry, and even pottery, whose only sound was the creaking of the potter's wheel.

A professor in the Visual Arts department at the University of Chicago—and recipient of the Artes Mundi 6 Prize and the Nasher Prize for sculpture—Theaster Gates is a multidisciplinary artist specializing in land development, sculpting, and performance. While his works often center on space theory and, in many cases, convey an interest in Black space, Gates is also known for capturing the life within materials and "things". Such an inner life played a massive role in the rejuvenation of the Temple Church, where Gates—with the aid of AN Architecture and arts organization Situations—built a structure using components and raw materials native to Bristol. Though most of the materials, construction, and planning of the main event were completed by the co-organizers and other UK-based figures, Gates masterminded the entire structure. His co-organizer Claire Doherty from Situations described Gates as having "very strong aesthetic control," and likened him to "a theatre director, where—once it's running—he leaves it in our hands." But Gates did more than orchestrate. He had a part to play in the twenty-four-day soundscape, taking to the Sanctum stage and singing an array of hymns unaccompanied—which had a disconcerting effect on the audience due to its deviation from convention and expectation, as told by *The Spaces* online magazine.

The structure in which *Sanctum* was held took two years and a diverse range of materials to build —remnants of Georgian houses, bricks donated by The Salvation Army, floors reclaimed from a former Bristol chocolate factory. Commenting on the materials he uses in his works, Gates proclaimed in an interview with Doherty that "they have something extremely sacred in them that might be sleeping, or may have been put into a coma, but is living, and we have to find ways to activate the living." This admission is particularly significant considering the revival of the Temple Church, where a forgotten place of congregation and worship is restored once more into a home of community and music.

In pioneering these projects in the name of social development, Gates is known for redeeming—and injecting with new life—spaces that have been left behind. In the case of *Sanctum*, the aim was "to bring the city together with music and sound." But, more than this, Gates wanted to focus on supporting local artists who, in his words, "live at the margins of Bristol who are making great music ... whether it's the Pakistani community or Punjabi-speaking folk, or West Indians or Nigerians, or the Scottish harmonica player." In this way, the *Sanctum* public art event achieved inclusion in the eyes of the public—who were able to easily access the performance at literally any time of the day for twenty-four days—and cultural diversity in the artists hired. And so, a structure frozen in history came alive again.

Dubbed by Artnet as "the poster boy for socially engaged art," Gates has worked on a plethora of other socially motivated public art projects besides *Sanctum*. Gates' Dorchester Projects, his most widely acclaimed work, saw the transformation of several buildings in the

Dorchester area of Chicago into cultural spaces, which facilitated workshops, performances, and even hospitality services, to enhance community development. Likewise, Gates repurposed numerous materials to refurbish the structures and circulated some 14,000 books from a closed-down bookstore.

KEHINDE WILEY—SCULPTURES THAT COUNTERPOINT POSITIONS

Kehinde Wiley is an artist who believes in the value of adding to and not erasing history. He finds such expression in correcting imbalances through his art and has recently invaded public spaces with his work. At the beginning of 2021, Wiley's stained-glass triptych *Go* was unveiled at the Moynihan Train Hall with artworks from two other artists. The triptych depicts several young, Black figures, adorned in streetwear and dancing across a vivid blue sky, frozen in breakdance-like positions. While the decidedly modern models celebrate Black youth in society today, *Go* decorates the top of the Moynihan Train Hall in style reminiscent of eighteenth-century frescoes. One woman in particular, whose arm is outstretched, her finger frozen in a point, echoes the *Creation of Adam*: the Michelangelo masterpiece that spans the ceiling of the Sistine Chapel in the Vatican.

Indeed, Wiley's career has been characterized by his reimagining of artworks from history. He frequently takes inspiration from the paintings of the old masters, only this time substituting contemporary Black figures for the White powerful or influential individuals of the day and allowing Black people to assume their place in a period of art history that had previously eluded them.

Wiley's most famous work of this nature is a portrait of Barack Obama, in which the forty-fourth president is seated against a backdrop of ornate greenery-inspired wallpaper. Though this particular genre is set in the convention of highlighting people of influence, many of Wiley's portraits depict ordinary people who have no specific distinction and challenge our notion not only of race but of the glorification of violence.

One of Kehinde Wiley's most recent, groundbreaking artworks is *Rumors of War*, a bronze twenty-seven-foot-high sculpture of a proud, hoodie-wearing Black man atop a horse carved in Renaissance fashion. Using the same historical style, Wiley challenges the traditional concept of race and power accorded to militaristic leaders on horseback in a pose suggestive of a battle cry. Wiley has engaged with the equestrian tradition in statues numerous times by uplifting Black figures and challenging historical biases about race.

The strange thing is that *Rumors of War* is the first time Wiley transferred this ambition to sculpture. Making use of artistic license, *Rumors of War* places the young Black rider on horseback in a position of power that he would not have had access to historically. So, ironically, Wiley complies with the historical conventions of form and style—like most of his artworks—yet criticizes the historical traditions and social context they are aligned with.

This equestrian sculptural tradition remained a

popular way of celebrating military figures from the Renaissance until the mid-nineteenth century with the defeat of the Confederate army. Before this, several equestrian statues created to honor Confederate army generals had been placed on Monument Avenue in Virginia, the former Confederate capital. The timing of these statues coincided with the rise of Jim Crow, one of the most influential advocates of racial segregation. A few years before *Rumors of War* was conceived, the artist witnessed these monuments in person for the first time. This had an immense effect on him, as he states in an interview with CBS, like being "in a black body walking through the streets of Richmond, and [seeing] something that signifies the enslavement of my people."

In particular, the sculpture of General Jeb Stuart was the monument that both inspired and provoked Wiley to create a sculpture that mimics and challenges the general's image. The Black figure shown in *Rumors of War* is in the same pose as Jeb Stuart, breathing the same warrior spirit into the monument while delivering a starkly contrasting message. Wiley imagines his sculpture "speaking back to the people looking at those statues." In his view, rather than having the Confederate statues taken down—as Richmond Mayor Levar Stoney advocates—responding to them with more sculptures that speak positively to our time and our sociocultural progression is the best course of action. In essence, Wiley asserts that the United States should not try to erase and rewrite its history, but rather to acknowledge and respond to it with art showing other perspectives. Unveiled to the public for the first time in Times Square in 2019, the permanent home of *Rumors of War* is on the grounds of the Virginia Museum of Fine Arts (VMFA), which is only a few blocks away from its counterpart on Monument Avenue.

SIMONE LEIGH—MERGING ARCHITECTURE WITH THE HUMAN BODY

Another African American artist who challenges historical stereotypes about race through sculpture is Simone Leigh. As a multidisciplinary artist who has worked with sculpture, video, and performance, Leigh has received numerous awards such as the Hugo Boss Prize and the Foundation for Contemporary Arts Grants to Artists award in 2018. Like Wiley, Leigh has a keen social interest that influences the content of—and the messaging behind—her work. She simultaneously pulls inspiration from historical art styles and mediums. She uses these same styles to challenge the marginalization of women of color, lifting them through her artworks to a more conceptually important place in society.

In her biography on the Foundation for Contemporary Arts website, Leigh reveals that she came to her artistic practice via philosophy, cultural studies, and a strong interest in African and African American art. This has imbued her work "with a concern for the ethnographic, especially the way it records and describes objects." Leigh is particularly interested in Black female subjectivity and draws inspiration from Katherine Dunham and Josephine Baker's figures.

Leigh uses sculpture to call attention to the strength,

power, and beauty of Black women. In *Brick House*, she subverts the historical expectations of the art medium—by depicting a woman of color—with African cultural and architectural influences. The sixteen-foot-tall sculpture portrays the head and torso of a Black woman—the torso appearing dome-shaped like the walls of a clay house, sturdy and robust, with a ridged skirt decorating the sides. Cornrow braids and cowrie shells trim the ends of her hair, and her dark skin is illuminated by the New York sun. Significantly, the sculpture is eyeless, as if to represent a Black "everywoman." It's a ceramic triumph—the culmination of the artist's expertise with clay and ceramics, a medium she fine-tuned early in her career, though on a much smaller scale.

While *Brick House* is undoubtedly a celebration of Black women, it is no less a tribute to Leigh's interest in architecture. It's the first sculpture in a series, named *Anatomy of Architecture*, which explores the merging of architecture with the human physique. When designing *Brick House*, Leigh was influenced by an array of architectural styles, predominantly African—most notably the *teleuk* beehive structures from Cameroon and Chad. According to the High Line website, she also takes inspiration from the architecture of Benin and Togo and from architectural muses as close as Mississippi.

Simone Leigh's proposal, detailing her ambition to create *Brick House*, was chosen from among the submissions of fifty other artists to be the first commission for the High Line plinth—a location in New York's relatively new High Line park—three years before the sculpture's unveiling. Cecilia Alemani, who was heavily involved in the selection of art for the space, stated in an interview with Vice that they "wanted to invite artists to create something that could hold this space and every other traditional piazza in Europe has a monument in the middle; we appropriated that concept to create a plinth or pedestal that is installed in the center of the space." The plinth has been installed with the largest seating area in the whole of the High Line park. Alemani goes on to explain that they want people to use the space as a place to gather, to spend time, and to converse, while others involved with the project hope for an even more comprehensive range of functions: to dance, to listen to music, and to view art in its many forms. This mirrors what Dominic Chambers stated in *The Black Market*: "In his mind, a good artist can make interesting works. They can hold an audience's attention for a certain period of mind. The great artists, however, can make interesting art while being conscious about their subjectivity and relationship with the world around them. Great art isn't just about the aesthetics; it is a highly critical intellectual activity." Accompanying the sculpture's unveiling and the opening of the final section of the park was a performance by Toshi Reagon with her composition *I Walk the West Side Line*, highlighting the multidimensional purpose of the space. Considering the monumental nature of Leigh's work, it is no wonder that the artist received the first-ever commission to create artwork for freedom, which is set to present the public with a new creation every eighteen months.

While the value of public art can often be overshadowed by the prestige of galleries, museums, and coveted collections, there is no doubt that public art is becoming an integral part of the art world and society. Being uniquely accessible, it is there for any kind of person to discover, enjoy, and potentially learn from. Black artists have something remarkable to give to the world of public art. With such a platform, these artists can reach infinitely more diverse viewers, spread positive messages about Blackness, challenge outdated ideas and conventions surrounding specific art forms, and elevate a community through the sharing of art.

SANFORD BIGGERS' ORACLE AS A MASTERPIECE OF PUBLIC ART

On the May 5, 2021, Sanford Biggers' exhibition at the Rockefeller Center opened to the public, in the first event in which a single artist has taken over the entire complex with their work. The exhibition was headed by an enormous twenty-five-foot tall bronze sculpture titled *Oracle*, the latest in the artist's *Chimera* series and the largest of Biggers's works to date. The bronze sculpture, weighing approximately fifteen thousand pounds, depicts a figure whose bottom half is reminiscent of the Statue of Zeus at Olympia—one of the Seven Wonders of the Ancient World—while the disproportionately large head pays homage to the artistic traditions associated with African masks, blending the different cultural and artistic traditions of antiquity.

As an art form, public art transcends the limitations of the traditional "art world," reaching beyond the sphere's usual audience—the regular gallerygoers who seek out the art experience at exhibitions or museums—to the everyman: people from a diverse range of backgrounds with diverging interests and occupations, who stumble upon the artwork fortuitously as they go about their daily lives, who become compelled to engage with it. Bearing this in mind, the medium of public art is a valuable catalyst for initiating societal conversations. It can reach a broader, more diverse audience than more traditional art spheres.

The artist notes that he took this into account while conceptualizing the work—the ideas for which began around ten years ago, with talks with the Art Production Fund for the current exhibit beginning about six years later—describing the gallerygoers and exhibition-goers as "insiders" who "already sort of know the premise, or some of the ideas behind, your work or they could easily find it out and have the tools to read it on a contemporary or art historical level." On the other hand, when contrasting this experience with the realm of public art, Biggers noted that when creating art for the public sphere, "you can't take any of that for granted."

However, the artists find it "amazing to watch" people interact with *Oracle* as a piece of public art. When visitors witness the sculpture at Rockefeller Center, it "could be the first time they've even heard of an Oracle," so they make judgments based on the "size, the scale, the color, the magnitude, the weight," notes Biggers. As such, the artist finds the comments and questions made by viewers fascinating, due to the absence of prior context informing their discussions.

While Biggers welcomes differing opinions—stating that, as an artist, "if everyone agrees in the positive or just the negative, then something hasn't worked"—he also emphasizes that misinformation is "not good." About *Oracle*, for example, the artist says that he had had to "speak out" when false claims were made that the piece was "a monument to African culture by New York City."

Uniquely, Sanford Biggers' *Oracle* can participate in these conversations as an interactive work that engages with viewers on Tuesdays and Thursdays from 3:00–4:00 p.m. Throughout Biggers's Rockefeller exhibition, where the artist has displayed a range of his works, there are QR codes by the art, which visitors can scan to unveil more information about the work in various media forms. The QR code accompanying QR the *Oracle* allows visitors to ask the Oracle a question. If the Oracle believes your question is worthy, they will respond with "mysterious, poetic vagaries," as Biggers summarizes in an interview with the *Art Newspaper*. In addition, various female celebrities will voice the Oracle's responses, as Biggers highlights, "almost all oracles were women."

As a work that "reference[s] various cultures and histories,"reconciling the artistic traditions of antiquity— namely, the Greco-Roman inspired body of Zeus and the oversized head inspired by African masks and sculpture— it also seeks to address the modern misunderstanding about these art forms. An Artnet article reported that Biggers felt "empowered to remix classical sculpture in part because our understanding of these forms is already so flawed," referring to the misconception that Greco-Roman sculptures were originally polished white marble when, in fact, they would have been brightly painted at the time of their creation and that the masks of African antiquity would have been beaded and pigmented, rather than black. These preconceptions result in that Biggers describes as "a white-washed version of the European objects and a black-washed version of the African objects." *Oracle*, by comparison, uniquely blends and reconciles the artistic traditions of cultures of antiquity, "talking to art history," as Biggers notes in one interview.

Throughout the artist's body of work, Biggers intentionally makes an effort "to make pieces that operate on several different levels," citing "the visual and the sensory" and, beyond this, the "historical, symbolic and cultural." Another example of this is the artist's use of cultural symbols, namely the lotus flower, an image that recurs in Biggers's works and that Biggers defines as "a symbol for triumph over tribulation." Biggers was first drawn to the lotus flower after his time in Japan and his studies of Buddhism. About the lotus flower, Biggers relays that it "comes from the muck and mire of a body of water and then rises to bloom into beautiful things." He relates this symbol to the experience of the African diaspora, who have transcended "the atrocities of abduction from Africa" to "live beyond the gravity of history." Fittingly, a lotus blossom is printed on the throne of *Oracle*, with each petal made up of the cross section of a slave ship, forming a uniquely blended cultural, historical element on the sculpture.

One of the most vital themes of Biggers' twenty-five-foot sculpture is mythology. The artist emphasizes that "the entire installation is based on mythology, narrative, and mystery," whereby the head and body celebrate Afrocentric and Greek myths, respectively. Since the Rockefeller Center is a hub of mythologically inspired artworks—such as the Zeus sculpture at the entrance of 30 Rock, the sculpture of Prometheus overlooking the ice skating rink, and the statue of Atlas on Fifth Avenue—Biggers is glad to have created a work with "a lot of African elements" as their newest companion in the space. The artist expands, saying that the sculpture feels as though it's "completing the rest of the story," verifying and drawing attention to an equally mythologically rich history as a representation of Afrocentric myth.

Moreover, the historical figure of the oracle—thought to be able to provide prophetic predictions and provide counsel and wisdom—was an international figure but most prevalently represented in Greek mythology. Despite the abundance of European elements present in *Oracle*, Biggers takes note of the lack of questions about the European features of the design and the surplus of questions about the aspects of African origin.

In recent history, the art world has facilitated "the proliferation of so many artists of color," as Biggers observes, and "Black art" and Black artists have risen to the forefront, even in media where Eurocentrism traditionally dominated as sculpture and public art. Over the last few years, artists such as Kehinde Wiley and Simone Leigh, for example, have reclaimed and subverted the expectations of the sculpture art form—which, historically, almost exclusively depicted White men—by depicting Black or Afrocentric figures. Likewise, with Biggers's contribution to the public art sphere, he adds another sculpture celebrating African culture and history, paying homage to these themes with the exaggeratedly large head, the sculpture's braids—a Maasai braid, which Biggers highlights are "usually used for his Maasai warriors"—that cascade down the figure's head and the mask-esque depiction of the face.

Biggers considers public art particularly as "a platform for so many voices of color from all around the world to speak." However, with the rise of multitudes of Black artists, who often respond to the Black experience with their art—both historically and contemporarily—Biggers highlights the importance of these artists "not replicating other people's voices and tone," elaborating that each artist should "seek to be a unique voice among a chorus of several others."

When asked about whether Sanford Biggers objects to his art being called "Black art," he says, "I try to avoid any of the labels as much as possible," which makes sense, considering the multifaceted, multicultural, multinational essence of *Oracle*. The artist himself classifies the sculpture as "black art . . . contemporary art . . . American art," highlighting that the work is more than one thing and can speak to a multitudinous audience. However, as a Black artist, about the Black community and other Black artists, when expressing themselves through their art, Biggers declares that he "wants our information, and our story—our diasporic story—to become the canvas."

Chapter 6

Making a Legacy of Portraiture

Elliot Barnes observes that in the past, portraiture was the privilege of the gentry, which illuminates why Blacks are notably absent in classical paintings, and divulges how he seeks to rectify that. The prominent Black portrait artists featured here take control of what it means, looks like, and feels like to be a Black person.

ELLIOTT BARNES—WHY FAMILY PORTRAITS MATTER

Elliot Barnes, the Paris-based architect, interior designer, and accidental art collector, is shaking up the art world with his growing collection of portraits. The collection comprises the likenesses of members of his family, works that he has commissioned from some of the most exciting young African American artists around today.

Though Barnes was born and raised in Los Angeles,

his orientation is principally European. He was educated at a French school, with his peers hailing from North Africa, Vietnam, Switzerland, and, of course, France. In addition to giving him "a different outlook on the world," his early education steered him toward his now home: Paris. From the young age of fifteen, Elliot Barnes knew that he wanted to move from the States to the city of love. He finally brought his plans to fruition in 1987, and he hasn't looked back since—unless you include the biannual trips to LA and the occasional New York detour.

Before leaving for Paris, Barnes received his education at Cornell University. There, he studied architecture and urban design, earning his bachelor's and master's during his six years of study. Barnes attributes much of his "intellectual and even sociological orientation" to Cornell. Still, far from wanting to revisit and relive those memories, Barnes, with the musing of a sentimental architect, says that he has no desire to see his college memories "torn down into something else," instead wanting to allow his memories to become romantic and fuzzy with age.

Elliot Barnes has always been interested in art, even in his early childhood years. His mother enrolled him in Saturday art classes at the Los Angeles County Museum of Art when he was about six years old. During this experience, he was even given the opportunity to meet Andy Warhol, who visited and worked with the kids there in the late 1960s. Barnes also recalls his mother never being able to throw anything away, being afflicted by the same "collecting bug" that has been imparted to his own art collecting. Likewise, the first photograph— his first artwork—he ever bought was from a professor for twenty-five dollars, and he still has it to this day.

At Cornell, Barnes was given a very Eurocentric education and, consequently, received thorough schooling on the Renaissance and Baroque style of art in addition to a few postwar artists. The Renaissance has particularly influenced the culture of art that permeates society today, especially the culture of art collecting.

Renaissance Influence

The Renaissance revived art and architecture. The artistic revolution in Italy was heavily patronized by the Medici, an affluent family residing in Florence who significantly impacted the arts and sciences. Florence's architectural landscape boasts the Medici Chapel, the Palazzo Medici, and the Uffizi Gallery, among others. Moreover, the Medici family directed most of the artwork created in Florence, as the artists of the day would typically work only on a commission basis.

In contrast, the artists of today typically create art of their own volition that is meaningful to them. As a result, art is usually purchased *after* its creation by an art enthusiast who can connect to that creation. I stated in *The Black Market* that "art collecting is emotional at its most basic level . . . " Barnes didn't understand the distaste artists had for the word "commission," and he gathered this was a "nasty word" for most artists. As Catherine McKinley stated in *The Black Market,* "I believe that it is important for collectors to keep in mind that every piece of art you buy is like buying a piece of an artist's soul and that being able to peer into that work and see their soul really matters for many artists." When Barnes first set out on a project, he was surprised to receive many rejections from insulted talents. He's since learned to rephrase his proposals, instead asking artists if they're available to take requests.

Yes, approaching artists is a delicate business. Barnes noticed that when you go to work with an artist, the artist "wants to know that you love them," a process that can be compared with dating. He notes that "artists are very unique individuals," which he is grateful for, as they can "bring a certain truth to our reality, and a certain point of view."

TRANSITION TO PORTRAITURE—BRINGING THAT BALANCE BACK

Barnes's arrival on the art collecting scene was quite serendipitous. When he left the States to begin his career as an interior designer in Paris for French designer Andrée Putman, this exposed him to celebrities in the art world, rubbing shoulders with some of the most exciting contemporary artists. One pivotal meeting was with George Condo, a highly sought-after contemporary artist. Soon after, Condo told Barnes to pick out any one of his artworks to keep for himself. He chose a piece, and from that point on, Elliot Barnes's art collecting journey truly began.

Not long after, Barnes was introduced by Andrée Putman to a woman named Claudia Gold, now curator at the Jewish Museum. She in turn introduced Barnes to her artist friends Kiki Smith and Andreas Serano, whom he sought and received artworks from. At this time, Claudia Gold was running "the artist space," where Barnes acquired more works from artists such as Carrie Mae Weems and Willy Cole. As his passion for art collecting developed, Barnes also rekindled his love for photography, adding to his collection. Barnes notes that when he spots an artwork he loves, he feels a "physiological change" and a physical need to have a piece, a typical characteristic of an art collector.

Around this time, Barnes met Demetrio Kerrison, an expert in the art collecting world, focusing on acquiring art from artists from the African diaspora. Barnes regards "Dee" as his mentor, while Kerrison describes Barnes as "amazing." In fact, Kerrison has been an enormous influence on Barnes's art collecting and the primary reason for the shift of interest toward the African American artist community. Before this shift, Barnes admitted that he had thoughts like, "Why can't I buy anything I like?" Over time, however, he pondered over the fact that the "scale was so tipped and imbalanced" against African American artists and people of color, and he realized that if there was a chance to "bring that balance back," then it was his duty to do so. As a result, Elliot Barnes now almost exclusively purchases art from people of color. His story reminded me of my conversation with Elan Nieves in *The Black Market*, who said, "Growing up, I found solace at the Metropolitan Museum of Art. The Met was a place of respite for me, but I never saw Black people as a focal point of the works on display. I felt they were consistently in the background, and so I began collecting pieces of my own, and became determined to address this."

As he became closer with Kerrison, Barnes was able to do an interior design show for *Architectural Digest* in Paris, and he posed the idea to Kerrison to "do portraits of all the men in his family." Barnes said that this was because usually, in French or Italian salons such as the one he was designing, there were always portraits of family members on the wall. He decided to do portraits of the men because only boys were born into the family. His mother had two sons, his brother had two sons, and Barnes himself has a son, so he thought that the portraits would be a marvelous way to document his family.

This project—now dubbed *The Barnes Contemporary*—transformed Barnes from an art-loving architect and interior designer into a respected art collector in his own right. However, he has never really considered himself one.

At the start of this project, Barnes commissioned emerging African American artist Kenturah Davis to paint six of these portraits. Davis is presently an artist in high demand, making Barnes's timing incredible lucky. The portraits were inspired by a Rudyard Kipling poem called "If" that Barnes's father had him and his brother learn when they were children and that Barnes likewise taught his son, making it its own kind of legacy as Barnes now intends the portraits to be.

A FAMILY LEGACY

To date, there are fifteen to twenty portraits in this

collection, all by African American artists. *The Barnes Contemporary* is meaningful from the perspective of an African American person in that, just as the Medici would document their existence by having portraits done, Barnes wants to do the same. Only later did he truly realize the importance of portraiture and what that meant in the Afro-American context. Barnes notes that people of color "achieved socioeconomic liberty" late, in a time where "people were painting less, and taking pictures more." Hence, there are relatively few portraits of African American people. *The Barnes Contemporary* is his way of saying, "Yes, my family exists, too," reclaiming a part of the past for the African American community that would have been inaccessible to them at an earlier time.

In contrast to the portraits painted at the height of their popularity, however, the Barnes family doesn't do sittings, in part because many of the family members he's had painted are no longer alive. However, that's not an issue, because through the use of modern technology, he can consult with artists over the phone and email scanned photographs of his family members.

Unlike Medici-funded portraits, Elliot Barnes doesn't intend for the project to flourish into a multimillion-dollar sensation—that simply "wasn't the point." He describes the project as "grassroots," an organic project he pursues for personal reasons. He doesn't even know if the project will be shown in his lifetime. Someone else in his family will need to carry on the torch to continue to develop the project, someone who has caught "the bug" that he and his mother seemed to share.

He may do an exhibition based on these portraits at some indefinite time in the future, but Barnes is uncertain whether the venue would be LA or Paris. At the moment, he has just launched @thebarnescontemporary on Instagram, to showcase the portraiture works withing the larger context of other works he has collected.

Right now, he says, "Black portraiture is hot," but this comes with limitations. "When you're walking into a room and you see a portrait of a Black person, it's immediately identified as Black art [or a] Black political statement," he notes, in what he sees that as a form of pigeonholing. In *The Black Market,* when Hill Harper spoke of "the art that slaves and their descendants created, he becomes even more lucid. He explains how the art world has tried to 'devalue something rather than just judging it for the piece of work as it is' by separating the works from all other art, labeling it either 'found art' or 'folk art' as if it were in a category other than fine art. As a collector, he is doing critical work to push back against this assault, the act of categorizing art properly—as art—his defense." Although Barnes may pivot to abstract art collecting, he will still do portraiture, and he found working with Yoyo Lander to produce one of the more recent portraits—one of his father—a "beautiful experience."

INSIDE THE LIVES AND WORKS OF THREE BLACK PORTRAIT ARTISTS: KERRY JAMES MARSHALL, HENRY TAYLOR, AND AMOAKO BOAFO

Portraiture can be as sterile as a headshot or as all-encompassing as an image of a person surrounded by the things that make them unique. Either way, a portrait is meant to memorialize a person—real or fictional—and impress another person with their presence. Portraits do more than provide us with an image of a person. They are intended to make us feel like we are being delivered a message from the person we're looking at. Although the message may be interpreted differently from viewer to viewer, that's what art is all about after all, isn't it? It isn't really about looking; it's about *seeing*. Essentially, portraits tell a story of a person from the eyes of the artist.

For the greater part of history, this kind of storytelling has been inaccessible to Black people; typically, it was White artists painting narratives about Black subjects. And as we've seen, Black people have historically been depicted in Western art as cartoonlike or in a manner that couldn't possibly come off as anything but derogatory.

But for the contemporary Black artist, it's time to assert one's identity as the subject. These three Black artists—Kerry James Marshall, Henry Taylor, and Amoako Boafo—have therefore wrested back control of what it means, looks like, and feels like to be a Black person through the portraits they paint.

It would be hard to discuss the styles these three men paint in without talking about some iconic portrait artists that influenced them.

Kerry James Marshall is a man who half admits he paints with a Picasso-like hand with blocks of color; he paints portraits from the waist up against solid or simple backgrounds; he even sometimes paints quite abstractly.

"It's negotiating the problem of what makes paintings complex," he told the *New York Times*, "on top of it, what makes artwork modern. And if 'modern' means in some way that the images become more fragmented and less clearly defined, then there's no way to escape the trajectory laid out by Picasso."

Many of Henry Taylor's portraits only depict his subject's face from forehead to chin, sometimes with the shoulders in view. Lucian Freud had a very similar style of painting. This allows the viewer to get up close and personal with the subject, perhaps leading them to ruminate on what they are thinking, who they are posing for, and who they are at the core.

Zadie Smith of *The New Yorker* wrote: "His greatest subject is the human personality, although, in his portraits, personality is not a matter of literal representation but rather a vibe, a texture, a series of vertical block colors laid out on a horizontal plane."

Amoako Boafo is a fresh-on-the-scene artist who paints with his fingers. The texture and patterns that he can create on canvas are not all that far removed from what is seen in many of Van Gogh's paintings—rough strokes and whirls of color used to create many of the scenes that are loved by people all over the world. Devon Van Houten Maldonado of the *Observer* wrote, "In Boafo's paintings of Black subjects, the skin is full of energy and alludes to more than Blackness, perhaps what's under the skin, as opposed to creating perfectly illustrative figures with a paintbrush, shadow, and highlights."

In order to authentically grasp the methodology and inspiration behind each of these artist's portraits, we will start by looking at who they are as individuals.

KERRY JAMES MARSHALL—AN EXPANSION OF BLACK IN ART

Kerry James Marshall was born in Birmingham, Alabama, in 1955. When he was a boy of just seven, his family moved to Watts, an area of Alabama that was rife with civil unrest. Their house was only blocks away from the Black Panther headquarters, and even as a young child, Marshall experienced—and sometimes was the victim of—violent crimes.

Despite the rough environment that Marshall grew up in, he still believed that anything was possible—and that's chiefly the story that he tries to tell through his art.

Marshall uses his portraiture to push back on the long-standing narrative that "Black is not Beautiful" (as mentioned by Thomas Jefferson in *Notes on the State of Virginia*). He does this not by pointing out that there is a lack of Black being represented as beautiful in art, but by producing as much art depicting Black beauty as he can. In *The Black Market*, I called Marshall "a true master of pictorial art, and nobody else has drawn the Black body with more elegance and authority."

"When you talk about the absence of Black figure representation in the history of art," Marshall told the *New York Times*, "you can talk about it as an exclusion, in which case there's a kind of indictment of history for failing to be responsible for something it should have been. I don't have that kind of mission. I don't have that indictment. My interest in being a part of it is being an expansion of it, not a critic."

Marshall was the first person in his family to attend college, which attests to his "anything is possible" way of thinking. In 1978, he graduated from the Otis College of Art and Design in Los Angeles and has since been featured in the Smithsonian, the National Gallery of Art, the Art Institute of Chicago, the Metropolitan Museum of Art, and dozens of other museums across America. Today, his paintings are selling for over 20 million dollars apiece at auctions. "When Kerry James Marshall's 1997 painting *Past Times* sold for $21.1 million at Sotheby's in 2018, it was a milestone for Black artists. Never had a painting by a living Black artist sold for so much money, and yet it was only the latest in a string of milestones that Marshall had set throughout his career," I said in *The Black Market*.

HENRY TAYLOR—AIMING FOR AUTHENTICITY

Henry Taylor was born the youngest of eight children in 1958 in Oxnard, California. His mother cleaned fancy houses for a living, and it was inside those houses that Taylor first encountered fine art. His exposure to paint as a medium came from his father, who was a commercial painter.

After high school, Taylor attended various community college classes including journalism, set design, and anthropology before he started work as a psychiatric technician at the Camarillo State Mental Hospital for ten years. During his time at the hospital, Taylor drew inspiration from patients whom he painted while studying for his BFA at the California Institute of the Arts. He painted on everything he could find, from cereal boxes to cigarette packs, bottles, and even furniture. No matter what he was painting on or with, his inspiration was always, *always* drawn from the people he saw in his journey through life.

"First of all, I love other people," he told Hamza Walker, the executive director of LAXART, in a recent conversation in *Cultured Magazine*. "I love to meet them, and the fact I can just paint them."

Taylor loves meeting and painting people so much that he will often invite them into his West Adams apartment in Los Angeles for a conversation, a drink, or a portrait session. These people come from all walks of life, are sometimes homeless, and are almost always Black. In these portraits, he tries to capture the subjects' authenticity, subjects who have little to no experience modeling. He asks them to sit, pays them for their time, and paints them. One example of this can be seen in his 2014 painting *You Really Gone Pay me to Sit?*, as said by the panhandler.

By contrast, Taylor also paints people from the art world (who are mainly White) and has an altogether different experience doing so. They appear to have a hard time sitting, as they are acutely conscious of how they are presenting themselves. This could detract from the spontaneity of the portrait.

Through this type of authentic portraiture, Taylor wants viewers to really *see* the people they're looking at on the canvas, rather them simply *looking* at them. He wants viewers to feel the emotion in the subject's eyes and create a narrative about the subject that comes from the heart, rather than a preconceived notion about whom and what they think they're looking at.

For example, one of his paintings depicts a little girl playing with a toy gun. It's titled *Girl with Toy Rifle*. Looking at this painting, you may see just that: a child with a toy rifle. But when you *see* it, you may realize the larger story it's telling: that children—Black children—also play with toy guns, and it doesn't make them any more dangerous or "grown" than their White counterparts.

Taylor's art is deeply rooted in the awareness that the Black experience in America, though unique, is not new. Many have found great success, though, despite starting at the bottom. But while some can achieve greatness, it is still not attainable for all. And that is the fact that Taylor wants to drive home so that we can fully see the reality of life.

Amoako Boafo—The Finger Painter

Amoako Boafo's story starts in Accra, Ghana, in 1984. His father died when he was young, so he was raised by his mother, a cook. While she worked, Boafo taught himself to paint at home, something that he thought would always be a hobby but never a career, because there are few opportunities in Ghana to pursue art professionally.

So, for many years, Boafo made a living as a semipro tennis player until one of the people who hired his mother as a cook paid for him to go to art school. In 2008, he graduated from Accra's Ghanatta College of Art and Design, where he won Best Portrait Painter of the Year. A few years later, in 2014, he moved to Vienna, Austria.

From there, Boafo's career skyrocketed, but not before he decided to paint with his fingers rather than paintbrushes. This unique aspect of his technique made him stand out from the crowd and gained him recognition from art enthusiasts throughout Vienna. The way that he painted Black skin made it seem as though it was coming to life, almost giving viewers a glimpse of vitality and energy radiating beneath the skin.

In 2018, Boafo's portrait of President Obama was purchased by a supporter of sub-Saharan African artists who subsequently contacted his networks in London, New York, Paris, and Los Angeles to let them know they had an emerging artist on their hands. From there, Boafo's portraits went on display in a gallery in Los Angeles, priced starting from $10,000 and dubbed as "magical" by the gallery owner.

Since that initial gallery exhibition, Boafo's art has been highly coveted worldwide, both for his unique style and for the mere fact that he paints Black portraits. This is even more true now with the Black Lives Matter movement exploding in 2020. Black art creations became à la mode. Boafo's highest-selling painting to date, *Lemon Bathing Suit*, was sold for $881,432 in 2019.

After that sale, his position in the art world was solidified. Today, he has a painting hanging in the Guggenheim—a massive victory for any artist, but especially for one so new on the scene.

Boafo is currently working on building an artist's residency in his hometown of Accra so that Ghanaians don't have to uproot and migrate to other continents to find opportunities in the professional art world.

Chapter 7

The Disruptors

Meet two artists who are intentional about creating work through novel media that can disrupt the status quo and make the audience wince or speak to something more primal and engaging.

NINA CHANEL ABNEY—TRANSCENDING CREATIVE BORDERS

Producing art that explores themes of gender, race, politics, and celebrity, Nina Chanel Abney uses abstract imagery to comment on contemporary culture and on the events and sociopolitical climate that influence the world each day. Of a style Abney describes as "easy to swallow, hard to digest," Abney's art is provocative and stimulating, and often veers toward the absurd, juxtaposing bold colors and cartoonish figures with the weighty themes and events she imparts.

Influenced by her mother's creativity, Nina Chanel Abney was always headed down the path of becoming an artist, graduating with a BFA in studio art and computer science before earning her MFA from the Parsons School of Design in 2007. It was here that critics and curators first recognized Abney's talent as she presented her MFA thesis titled *Class of 2007*. Alluding to the racial disparity within prisons as well as in her class—where she was the only Black student—*Class of 2007*, a fifteen-foot-wide diptych, recasts her White classmates as Black prisoners clad in orange jumpsuits, while Nina Chanel Abney reinvents herself as a White, blonde, armed prison guard, separated from the inmates by a border.

As an artist, Abney revealed that she's "intentional about creating work that gets a mixed response". And that was the exact reception that her thesis got on the day of her show. Abney noted that a number of her classmates were made "uncomfortable" by the portrait. She also admits that the person she thought would be made *most* uncomfortable by the flipped image, she had made "very dark-skinned," revealing her provocative intent.

As *Class of 2007* continued to cause a stir beyond the campus, it caught the attention of the Rubell family, art collectors and owners of a private museum in Florida. It ultimately became the cornerstone for the rest of Abney's career. From this vantage point, Abney was featured in the *30 Americans* exhibition that highlights the work of some of the most prominent African American artists living, Abney being the youngest artist to be featured.

Following a dazzling ten years in the art world, Abney earned her first solo museum exhibition, the *Nina Chanel Abney: Royal Flush*. It was displayed at the Nasher Museum of Art in North Carolina in 2017, then again in

2019 at the California African American Museum and the Institute of Contemporary Art in Los Angeles before finding a permanent home at the Neuberger Museum of Art in New York.

In addition to Abney's earliest curated work, *Class of 2007*, another of her most notable works, *Close But No Cigar*, is also featured in the collection. This is a work inspired by the assassination of Martin Luther King Jr. It reimagines the scene in an uncanny burlesque where Barack Obama—only a presidential candidate at the time of the painting's inception—can be seen lying on the floor wrapped in the American flag.

Although in the past Nina Chanel Abney often depicted specific, usually political events in her art—including violent representations of police brutality, as in the case of *Always a Winner*—this is a practice she has shifted away from, favoring "more abstract narratives, stripping away the backgrounds to take away specific meanings to latch onto." This is particularly noticeable in many of her recent collages, as they force the spectator to derive a unique meaning and, therefore, become meaningful to them. For Abney, "every interpretation is welcome."

Abney reveals that she wants viewers to have a "personal relationship" with her artwork, so she tries to avoid being pigeonholed or associated too strongly with one particular cause or message. By making the events and figures depicted in her work somewhat inscrutable, she accomplishes open interpretability for the most part, though she admits that, if she paints a Black figure, "it can't just be a figure." Like it or not, her work is often seen as a commentary on race and racial issues. This is something that White artists "don't have to think about," she finds. Likewise, she avoids giving direct answers to questions that attempt to pry open the meaning behind her work, preferring to maintain the enigma surrounding her abstract, figurative images. Rather than interpreting the art she creates and providing her viewers with a pre-packaged message, Abney prefers to have people ask themselves questions "about race, gender, and identity" in response to her artwork and to elicit "multiple reactions, not just one."

In 2020 Abney opened up the discussion between artist and viewer for the first time, breaking through the barrier that ordinarily separates the two parties by combining her artistry with the technological capabilities of augmented reality (AR). Named *Imaginary Friend*, Abney's AR creation was launched in collaboration with *Acute Art in 2020*, inspired by Abney's experience with lockdown and isolation.

Abney describes *Imaginary Friend* as a "talisman" or "good luck charm," as it takes the form of a sage or deity who attempts to bestow a blessing onto a friend. When this blessing is rejected, the sage interacts with the viewer and says, "sometimes we believe nothing good can ever happen to us, so it doesn't." While artwork can also be considered like a fairy godmother, the benevolence of this figure can be subverted, suggesting that the viewer can only make a positive change—and therefore be helped—if they believe that change is possible. Abney describes *Imaginary Friend* as an "always-ready companion" to aid those struggling with the uncertainty and precariousness of life in the present. In an interview with the *New York Times*, she described it as an offering "to anyone who's suffering right now," and she has made *Imaginary Friend* accessible in miniature form through the Acute Art app so that, even though many people are still in isolation, they, too, can receive comfort.

As a versatile and adaptable artist, Nina Chanel Abney has evolved through the different stages of her career as a creator and an innovator, sailing through various media and materials and resisting the tendency to be typecast in a particular role or by a certain aesthetic. As a result, she has produced paintings, collages, diptychs, prints, and more, with her works being displayed worldwide. At her exhibition *Hot to Trot. Not* (2018) at the Palais de Tokyo in Paris, Abney even produced temporary murals on the walls of the main stairwell, reinforcing the image of an artist who transcends the need for a specific platform, material, or medium. Abney further transcends the boundaries of fine art and translates her work to other media, allowing her art to become more accessible to— and hence enjoyed by—the masses by collaborating with a brand manager and other creators and artists.

Using some of her hallmark designs, Abney has produced T-shirts with bold colors and enigmatic, powerful messages, while her limited-edition dolls, some priced at $850, sold out in seconds.

Abney is also the latest artist to partner with Mattel in the *UNO Artiste* series. Abney is the third artist to do so, following Jean-Michel Basquiat and Keith Haring, an artist that Abney herself has been compared to in the past and who she states inspired her to extend her practice beyond the canvas. The 112 UNO cards in the deck feature a unique design executed in Abney's bold, unapologetic style, which she hopes will heighten the game's intensity due to the provocative images and a bonus "No" rule card, innovated by the artist herself.

Furthermore, in collaboration with Joe Tavares and Google, Abney has worked to produce phone cases that showcase some of her most recognizable and spectacular images. This is a remarkably suitable medium for Abney's art, as many of the symbols used in her work are inspired by emojis and the notion of using just a single symbol to communicate.

Refusing to restrict herself to just one material, medium, message, or cause, Nina Chanel Abney explores the universes of fine art and commercial art as she embarks on a mission to share her art through every medium necessary to find—and provoke—her audience.

Laolu Senbanjo—Storytelling on Skin

Human rights lawyer and activist, performing and visual artist—colloquially known as Laolo NYC—the Nigerian-born Laolu Senbanjo infuses his heritage into every aspect of his work. This New York–based creator incorporates what he calls Afro Hysterics into his varied pieces, weaving African proverbs, thought patterns, and symbolism throughout the buildings, walls, textiles, and bodies that he uses as canvases.

Before arriving in Brooklyn in 2013, Senbanjo spent three years practicing law in his native Nigeria, where he admits he became intensely aware of his own privileged life. As a senior legal officer for the country's National Human Rights Commission, he oversaw the implementation of the Child's Right Act. He quickly learned how devastating Sharia law could be for women in particular, with girls in their early teens forced into marriage. Senbanjo knew he wanted to help change the broken structures he faced each day. But how? Either make a limited impact as a human rights lawyer or make a grander impact by building public awareness as an artist. In his words, there was a "raging beast" inside of him—and by unleashing that beast, he could embrace his true self and serve Nigerians on a global scale.

Outside of Africa, most people tend to make a sweeping generalization of Africans, to Senbanjo's frustration. Nigeria, for example, is home to over five hundred language groups. Forty million people speak his native tongue, Yoruba, which he believes to be the fountain of his life. Yet far too many people have a shallow understanding of Africa and see it as a monolith of sorts (an unfortunate consequence of colonization). This couldn't be further from the truth. The continent is rich in diversity by tribe, culture, geography, and history, although under British rule the people were forced to be assimilated into the Western patriarchal system. The nations' emerging consciousness is a painful, *gradual* process even after most African nations have long gained independence. Nonetheless, there is a sense of collective awakening as Africans rise up to claim their unique heritage.

Senbanjo's choice has paid off well. Since he arrived in

New York eight years ago, he has collaborated with giants like Nike, Starbucks, Bvlgari, Alicia Keys, and Beyoncé. The collaboration with Beyoncé featured several parallels with Vanessa Beecroft and Kanye West's *Runaway* video. For Senbanjo, working on Beyoncé's 2016 film *Lemonade* and her song *Sorry* was a surreal experience. This exposure not only propelled Senbanjo into fame but allowed him to infuse the performance with Yoruba practices. He explains that Beyoncé's team reached out to him intending to create something reminiscent of Creole culture, and the Yoruba people—whose lineage is, in fact, Creole—fit perfectly. His work based on the Yoruba's *Sacred Art of the Ori* drew Beyoncé to the spiritual, sacred tenets she hoped to explore.

But more remarkable than being associated with an international icon was that the choreography, music, and body art in the making of that video deeply resonated with Senbanjo. What greater opportunity to share his culture with hundreds of millions of people after having that same culture stolen or put on the back burner in so many ways! And so, Senbanjo painted his Orisun art onto the faces and bodies of Beyoncé's dancers, inviting intrigued audiences to participate in his culture.

Senbanjo dreams of starting a foundation in Nigeria to provide art materials to local young talents, and he already supplies artists with pens whenever he returns home. Just as he left his law practice for a wider field, Senbanjo is committed to increasing access and opportunity for those who lack the means.

"Everything is my canvas," he states in conversation and on his website. Bodies, cologne bottles, packaging—

the artist finds inspiration everywhere he looks. He takes mundane objects, textiles, and the human form, and he clothes these elements with the African mystique. Often, Senbanjo paints on leather, a surface he once considered impossible to paint on. He starts by dabbing the material with a piece of cloth, wiping it down, and replacing the factory extras with his designs. Today, the artist works mainly with silk screen on canvas, using indigo-blue fabric, another vital component of Yoruba culture.

The painting on skin is an effort to represent his ancestors, for each time his subjects touch their skin, Senbanjo explains, they are connecting with the spirits of those who walked before him. Working with models to bring these images to life, he may spend fourteen hours painting their skin before having them sit for a photograph. He subsequently wanders to his computer and browses the thousands of pictures he's taken, saving the selects, creating the screen afterward, and then going through different backgrounds composed of various layers of blue. Adding a delicate layer of 24-karat gold here, he draws on the screens and then dives into the leafing process before starting again. There are multiple layers of color involved in this collaborative effort in which the models, or subjects, become the art and essentially wear Senbanjo's creations on their skin.

Senbanjo traces this style of mark-making back to his early days in the art space, when he'd paint his clothes to spark conversation and generate commissions. He would paint on shoes and jackets, covering the material with his designs, creating his gallery of sorts, and people would approach him to see if they could commission their own.

The artist would talk to them, ask them for their own stories, and then tell each person's history in his artistic style. Senbanjo deems inquiry essential to stirring the creative interests of the young.

All this ties in with the current generation, as the artist emphasizes how tired many viewers claim to be of simply seeing pieces staring back at them. People are hungry for engagement, for involvement. And, by telling their stories on their skin—through Senbanjo's lens—they can elevate their history, while the artist can share the essence of his own culture and story.

ALTERONCE GUMBY—HORIZON CONVERGENCE (2021)

For the last year, emerging New York artist Alteronce Gumby has been contemplating his latest geometric piece, *Horizon Convergence* (2021), a massive 96-by-156-inch abstract canvas composed of two large rectangles stacked off-center, reminiscent of the solar system. The painter, who graduated from Yale's MFA program in 2016, views the piece as something of a conversation with the great heroes of abstract expressionism: Mark Rothko and Barnett Newman, Jackson Pollock, and Philip Guston. From the time Gumby first set foot in the Museum of Modern Art—back in 2008, he recalls—he experienced an overwhelming desire to engage with these abstractionists. *Horizon Convergence*, which features gemstones, painted glass, and acrylic on panel, allowed him to be a part of the canon. In his words, the piece permitted Gumby to speak at the same volume as the greats.

To bring *Horizon Convergence* to life, Gumby maxed out his studio wall space—in an effort to be as ambitious as possible with his glasswork, he carefully applied gemstones as large as his fist onto the panel. The artist's objective was to make a real impact. In the same way, his expressionist idols influenced his own life and work, and again, to make sure he could communicate everything he wanted to say, ensuring the work resonated at the highest possible frequency. Gumby considered the history of shaped paintings for the duration of the piece's creation, considering Ellsworth Kelly's linear approach in addition to the vibrant shapes of Sam Gilliam and Al Loving's geometry. Rather than mirroring existing works, the artist set out to craft an entirely new shape, which could propel him into what many would consider an entirely new dimension.

Ask Gumby about the idea behind the work, and he'll tell you he was thinking of cosmic landscapes, the movement of the planets, and the essence of the galaxy as a whole. His objective was to squeeze the vastness of the solar system into a single painting, with minerals and elements that evoke an almost extraterrestrial sense of fascination: human beings are so small, and yet everything is connected, right down to our collective spiritual essence and all that we cannot see. *Horizon Convergence* is black and brilliant, highlighting the deepness of space, contrasting the small and the large, the minuscule and the maximum. The fragmented gemstones and colored glass culminate in a meditative effect, allowing viewers to align themselves with the cosmos—just as the piece's title conveys.

By definition, horizon convergence is a phenomenon that occurs when all of the planets in the solar system line up; in certain cultures, it is thought to cause a sort of peak energy in which certain spells or intentions can materialize seemingly from thin air. According to Gumby, the purpose behind the piece, in addition to the abovementioned conversation with legendary expressionists, is simply to *manifest*. From left to right, the piece features black tourmaline—the stone of protection, meant to ward off harmful spirits (more specifically, tourmaline is a hexagonal crystal sourced from the aluminum borosilicate family, blending magnesium, iron, and other metals, found on every continent in the world)—camouflaged to create an aesthetic delay when the glass is observed, mixed with a bit of blue to enhance the meteoric pigment Gumby likes to use. The artist reminds the public there are actual elements from the cosmos he incorporated into the work. From there, *Horizon Convergence* showcases pulverized coral, coral reef, and a quartz cluster meant to focus intention and increase clarity. (Quartz, Gumby says, has the effect of a natural battery, powering watches and giving off the highest frequencies within the gemstone family.) Quartz's relationship to the sun is unparalleled, and the artist proudly conveys that it's almost as if his piece is solar-powered through the mindful use of energy-based gems. There's the amethyst to keep toxicity at bay, and there's a second coral cluster (aurora this time) with the same textural power as the first. There's more coral, an aurora quartz cluster, and then additional quartz and amethysts scattered throughout the canvas; the black tourmaline again serves to punctuate the piece, which ends on the right side with a final piece of quartz.

The painting exudes the appeal of a low-relief landscape, with tremendous yet ambiguous galactic vistas set against the rawness of the gemstones. There's a unique blend of movement and energy—a unique sense of power designed to highlight the artist's relationship with the atmosphere, and by proxy, with the viewer's overarching sense of spatiality. Despite the black tourmaline and the coral, the chunks of obsidian volcano glass, and smaller pieces of activated minerals like malachite and zeolite, the work is cohesive; each small piece works *with* the rest rather than in opposition to it. The gemstones' frequencies bounce off one another, creating a charged effect that Gumby claims uplifts him just from standing before it. It's meant to be a return to astronomy class, a visit to the planetarium, as though gazing at *Horizon Convergence* could cut the lights, close the roof, and put the entire solar system on display. The piece is fragmented and glowing, creating an immersive experience that will take the viewer's breath away as they work to ingest it all: observing it, assessing the energy of the work, and contextualizing the gems placed upon the dark, vast panel.

Though all-encompassing, Gumby reminds the public that *Horizon Convergence* is meant to be taken in alongside a smaller piece entitled *Golden Chords* (2021). The latter was created in conversation with the former, blending layers of fragmented glass and pieces of malachite, golden nuggets embedded into the work to map out the artist's Libra sun sign. Gumby refers to *Golden Chords* as an embedded constellation of sorts—he returns time and again to this striking planetary theme—or even an astrological self-portrait. The piece features some of the original glass the artist sourced from a bus stop, the same place from which he began his glasswork years ago. It's a reference to his personal history, Gumby explains. And again, there's a pull that draws the viewer right in. With the painting's brilliance, the black and the gold, the smoothness, and the tiny, sharp shards, it becomes challenging to look away.

Chapter 8

The Eclectics

What motivates an art collector? How does a collector select artwork? What first stirred their fascination with art? As an artist or art enthusiast, it can be interesting to learn what pushes others to invest in art pieces and to learn the story behind their relationship with art. Here are fresh perspectives and insights from three collectors.

VICTORIA ROGERS—A LOVE FOR STORIES AND RELATIONSHIPS

Victoria Rogers is an enigma of sorts. Although the thirty-year-old Brooklyn Museum board member's art collecting is rooted in a familiarity with the arts from that began she was very young, like most collectors, she has a unique twist to her collecting experience. As a young art collector, Victoria is a member of a new generation of collectors who are the vanguard of a refreshing break from the historically "mature" nature of art collecting. But there's more. She also enjoys an intimate relationship with art, having grown up making art—unlike many other collectors. Victoria's insider experience with art, both as a board member on art institutions and as an artist in her youth, together with over ten years of collecting art, place her at an interesting intersection as an art collector.

Born to Desiree Rogers, former White House social secretary, and John W. Rogers Jr., founder of Ariel Investments, Victoria became immersed in the art world at a young age, making doodles and squiggles at the dinner table before her parents caught onto her interests and enrolled her in art classes at school. While she soon realized that her talents might lie more strongly someplace other than art, Victoria admits that her experience with making art has become integral to the values that shape her art collecting.

She says, in an interview with *Cultured Magazine*, "I grew up making art in Chicago in a family that was very supportive of my interests. But I realized pretty quickly that I was not an awesome artist, so I instead looked for opportunities to be close to those who are. I think that for me especially—as someone who tried to make art as a young person—I appreciate the craft and how difficult art-making can be. Collecting was actually a second chapter to my involvement with museums." That early exposure also set the tone for what is turning out to be a significant art collecting and professional career.

How did it all begin? Victoria's first art purchase was largely accidental. According to Victoria, the acquisition started out innocently enough with her research on Sotheby's for a high school economics research project. She attended an auction at the prestigious house with her father in 2010, and she ended up acquiring Émile Bernard's *Vue de Pont-Aven*. These days, her tastes in art are much more defined, and while she agrees that "it's very random, especially considering my interest now," you never really forget your first acquisition.

"Every work has a story behind it," says Victoria. For her, the experience of collecting is really about trying to understand the stories that underlie these works. A notable part of that is letting her heart take the lead when it comes to collecting. She says, "I think for me, that it's really from the heart." As she explained to the *New York Times*, "I fall in love with things and collect them without a grand strategy. They also all have a deeper story, where I am supporting a friend, or connecting to a personal relationship or a cause beyond the aesthetic object."

In her own way, Victoria seeks to identify with the artists and their stories, especially from an African American, gender-relevant, and cultural perspective. "I collect African American artists, pretty much. Exclusively women, a couple of women who are not African American identified. I try to be pretty focused, if that is the right word." Victoria supports people who have traditionally been excluded from the art world and people like her who need to be reflected in our culture.

This also hints at how Victoria prefers to collect her art. Rather than focus on collecting abstract or figurative works or working through art advisors to unearth the latest gem, Victoria prefers to work through Instagram and galleries to build relationships with the artists themselves. She says, "Most of my work has been figurative, but . . . it's more about the artists and having a relationship with them than it is about the quality. I really view it as being a part of their story and being just a part of their work."

Victoria has had a great deal of involvement with art institutions and the cultural community as well as art-related capacities in other places. She was a director of arts at the crowdfunding platform Kickstarter and currently occupies board positions at the Brooklyn Museum and public art organization Creative Time. For Victoria, her position as the youngest member on these boards member helps her bring a unique perspective that allows the institutions to think more "digitally and innovatively." As mentioned already, a sizable sect of the art collecting and art worlds can get "stuffy," and the fresh perspectives of the new generation of art connoisseurs can lend modernity and creativity to these institutions.

Part of the vital work she is doing at the Brooklyn Museum involves cochairing a board committee that oversees diversity, equity, inclusion, and access at the institution. According to Victoria, the committee works to bring on more diverse artists and employees and attract more diverse visitors. "Our mission is to create a museum of diverse perspectives," Victoria stated, and this includes focusing on members of staff, their artists, and the people they work with, and it also extends to those in the community and the people they bring into the institution.

For all collectors, there's a point when you need to start asking how you want to manage your collection and what legacies you hope to leave behind. But part of the benefits of collecting so young is that there is a wealth of time to find a niche in the community and build things out at a steady pace. Victoria is taking things one step at a time, although one thing that remains dear to her is sharing her artworks with other people and institutions, at least through loans at the moment. "I have right now four different works that are out on loan. For me, it feels like a lot saying it. The most exciting thing is to be able to see an artwork that you've taken care of getting to be a part of a bigger story. For me, it's been a rewarding part of being an art collector. And I really just see myself as someone who is helping to shepherd something along and care for it. And, yes, to have it shared with more people is really a gift and something I always say yes to."

What advice does she have for others like her who are looking to flesh out their collections? "I would say really just follow your heart in terms of who you believe in, and share your values."

KENT KELLEY—PROTECTING AND PRESERVING THE CULTURE

Growing up around art, Kent Kelley watched his mother create charcoal paintings before he could fully understand the process. Although his art appreciation had not yet fully blossomed, he recalls that there were aspects of art that he relished even then; it was seeping into his consciousness, defining his character and personality, and shaping the person he would become. It was fun for him to watch what his mother was doing, to witness the flow state that she entered whenever she was painting and the peace that she experienced when expressing herself creatively.

From a foundation of those early experiences, Kent set off on a lifelong journey in the world. Unfortunately, his mother passed away when he was only fourteen years old, and the self-taught artist left behind no works that he could hang on his wall. Kent was left with only the memories that she instilled in him and the passion that she ignited.

In his twenties, Kent started to make purchases of his own. He picked up a couple of pieces, merely intending to decorate his home. But when the paintings were on his wall, he decided to do some more extensive research. Looking into the pieces he had bought, he found that the artist, Charles Bibbs, had already experienced a level of success, some of his work having been featured on *The Cosby Show*. The other artist, Susan Saint James, was also well known, which intrigued Kent to look into art further. He had stumbled upon an opportunity to learn and conduct research, immersing himself in the art world and resolving to see what else was out there. From the simplest of intentions, nothing more ambitious than the search for art to decorate his home, he had thrown himself back into the very passion that his mother had imparted to him when he was still a child.

In Oakland, Kent visited a Jack London Square gallery run by an older gentleman named Samuel. Samuel spoke at length about Charles Bibbs and Susan Saint

James, and soon after, Kent had purchased two of the Bibbs' pieces. One of the pieces, an original Bibbs sketch, he holds on to this day, but it was not until 2015 that he took up collecting in earnest. He started to think beyond the walls of his own home, understanding that there was something more that art could be—that if he put thought into what he was doing and planned out his acquisitions, he could turn his art collection into a legacy for himself.

As Kent puts it, "Doing research into different areas of art, I really tapped into this urban-influenced interest and that included everything, from either an artist who's from an urban background or even just struggles—the whole art influenced by the struggles in life, and just liberation in general, and with, of course, the African and the African diaspora background."

Over the last five years, Kent has devoted himself to studying art. He has made it his mission to learn about artists, especially new ones, by attending museums, galleries, and fairs, as well as by reading. In addition, he spends a significant portion of his time researching art and artists online, figuring out which of the galleries best match his goals and preferences. From there, he connects with gallerists, listening when they speak about the art market landscape and meeting influential people and other collectors.

At the core of Kent's mindset as a collector is his own taste. The question "Does the work appeal to me?" always defines his thought processes. When he purchases a piece of art, he wants to know that it appeals to him personally and that it is something he wants on his walls, not simply that the artist's name carries cachet or that other people are collecting that type of art.

Kent cites two people who have influenced him as a collector more than anyone else. Nyama Wingood sold him one of his first fine art pieces after he took up collecting as a serious endeavor. The painting, a piece by Tim Okamura, became an opportunity for Nyama to induct him into the art world once more. Since, she has also introduced Kent to artists such as Nathaniel Murray Quinn, and Jerome Lagarrigue.

The second person, Karen Jenkins Johnson, has helped him navigate the art world, teaching him through her roles at the Jenkins Johnson Gallery and the Jenkins Project in New York. He says, "She is so well connected in the art world, just so knowledgeable, I reached out to her for advice on different things . . . and Karen's great because just even building my profile as a collector and thinking about how I should be thinking about my collection and about the long-term, Karen has just been phenomenal in terms of the advice that she provides there."

In his collection, Kent mentions multiple exciting pieces—exciting first and foremost because he appreciates the artists' work. He mentions several artists by name, including Kehinde Wiley, Asuka Anastasia Ogawa, and Vaughn Spann. Because of his connection to Nyama Wingood, he frequently hears about artists before they have broken through. Asuka Anastasia Ogawa is one such artist. "I just think she's a phenomenal artist that I believe is here for the long term and will have a phenomenal career."

Speaking about the styles within his collection, Kent says that he leaned more toward figurative art up to this point. However, as of late, he has opened himself up more to abstract art. "I think those figurative pieces are often just more accepted and initially appealing to you, but now I actually am exploring abstracts much more and also, I think there are a lot of abstract artists out there who don't necessarily get the appreciation that they deserve, and I think that that, to me, means undiscovered value."

To Kent, art collecting is an endeavor that is deeply meaningful and personal. Legacy, as he describes it, has become a multifaceted concept. He defines it at length: "Start with one, just protecting the culture and preserving the culture. That's so important to preserve the culture and to ensure that others are aware of it and the importance of it. As artists become successful, their work, unfortunately, is not always in the hands of the African community, or the African diaspora. So, one of the important things, too, for me in collecting is to ensure that is the case. Legacy, for me, is ensuring not only do I do that, but my family actually understands the importance of that. As I think about fast forwarding into time, that will also mean eventually, for me, I'm not in this to sell the work. Eventually, at some point, these will either be gifted or passed on to subsequent generations. Even those gifts, I want those gifts to reflect institutions that have a strong tie to the African and African diaspora so the work continues to be accessible to the community."

In the same vein, Kent is enthusiastic about joining a board and acting as a voice to protect and preserve "the culture." He says that he has made some progress toward finding a board seat. Once he is in a position of authority, it is clear that he knows how he would wield that authority, supporting institutions that make their art accessible to the public and empowering up-and-coming artists both as an advisor and as a collector.

Taking a look back at the five years that have passed since he began collecting art seriously, Kent emphasizes that for anyone who is just beginning themselves, it is critical to find pieces that they like and to focus on their tastes. Having had this mindset, Kent is able to examine the pieces he bought five years ago and still appreciate them, them being reminders of why art is engaging for him. He also recommends that new collectors take some time (two years or so) to educate themselves before they make any purchases and learn about African American artists and artists of the African diaspora by visiting galleries and shows.

Patience, it is evident, is an essential value for Kent. He states emphatically that serious collectors need to educate themselves about the market. Even his own education, he says, is rudimentary, and he estimates that it will take another ten years for his perspective to mature. Highlighting all the moving parts, from the businesspeople to the collectors to the advisors to the gallerists to the auctioneers, he adds, "It just takes time to understand all of those things but then also to know the people, right?" Recently, Kent has added an increasing interest in abstraction, purchasing a work by master artist Sam Gilliam and another work by Tariku Shiferaw.

From watching his mother paint in his youth, that patience, if his growing collection is any indication, has undoubtedly paid off.

Natassha Chambliss—Avid Print Collector

Natassha Chambliss's interest in art started at an early age and has only continued to prosper from there. Her journey to becoming an avid art collector started with the firm conviction that she was an artist herself. From an extremely young age, she was already drawing and creating her own coloring books. She finished store-bought coloring books so quickly that her mother decided to stop purchasing new ones. Natassha took this as a challenge and started creating pages on any and every white paper surface in sight. She was doing this from around five or six, and as she got older, she continued to pursue the arts in her studies.

Natassha attended Milwaukee High School of the Arts to study visual arts, photography, sculpting, painting, and drawing. This experience was extremely formative for her, as she spent much of her time during her junior and senior years in the Milwaukee Art Museum. During this time, she was able to sculpt and paint among artistic masters. For a little Black girl with a passion for the arts, this was a truly life-changing and humbling experience.

Although occupying these spaces was a privilege, she was quick to notice the absence of other Black artists; not only that, but there also seemed to be a blatant disregard for Black artists in museum spaces. It was rare to see a painting that depicted a Black person unless they were a servant or slave in an old-school oil painting. Even during the 1990s, it was rare to see incredible work created by Black artists, except for artists like Romare Bearden and a few others. A few years later, she would notice that Kehinde Wiley had *St. Dionysius* in a museum, a beautiful piece depicting a young Black man in a royal-blue puffer jacket holding a torch. It would be years until Natassha could see pieces that represented her in a museum setting.

This realization lit a fire under her and influenced her journey as an art collector. After many years, she put her artistry behind her and became a magnanimous supporter of artists, especially toward her friends who were creatives producing incredible pieces. She supports and champions the arts as a collector and volunteer, serving on boards for the arts. This is how she stays engaged and connected to the art world, spending copious amounts of time visiting museums and art shows.

The first official piece in Natassha's collection was acquired only three years ago: a woodblock from the artist Jamaal Barber. Jamaal is a printmaker who lives in Atlanta, where Natassha currently resides. The show Jamaal put on was called *Bright Black* and it featured many wood-release carving prints. Along with this, he included blocks and an entire book called *The Color Theory*. Throughout the book, he included pages with relief carvings. He also took components from old-school coloring education books like *Black Is Always Black* or *White Is the Absence of Color*. This series of relief works formed Jamaal's first solo exhibit.

Natasha was impressed when she attended the show. The pieces were more expensive than she could have ever expected, but her determination to obtain a piece was unwavering. Jamaal did a workshop where he produced a woodblock as a sample to demonstrate how he came up with the ideas for his large pieces. The artist decided to sell the piece to Natassha after making two prints, one for Natassha and one for himself. This piece is singularly special to Natassha because only she and the artist have the prints, and she is the only one with the actual block. Natassha continues to collect pieces from Jamaal. She also collects the blocks he uses for prints after each series is finished as well as the print.

"It's an addiction," she says of collecting. However, this addiction start long before she acquired her first work from Jamaal a few years ago. Over the years, seeing her grandmother and other family members decorate their homes with landscape art pieces from places like Walmart, Target, TJ Maxx, or Marshalls inspired her to do the same in her own home. After moving to Georgia, she was set on decorating her home with art to support her friends who are artists.

Collecting for Natassha isn't just about supporting her fellow creatives; it's also about educating herself on what's truly important in the art world. As a result, she took the initiative to start investing in especially art by young Black artists.

As she started to attend more and more shows almost every weekend, Natassha was exposed to an abundance of artwork. Although she couldn't always afford the pieces, she would get the catalogues from the show and read up on the works. She would then talk to friends and artists about their inspirations. They would often reference books, other artists that inspired them, or techniques they learned on their artistic journeys. From this, she read up on the types of art that captivated her. That happened to be woodcut and relief prints. These speak to her the most because they are entirely original and limited-edition pieces, and also are quite affordable.

As Natassha read more and more on the artworks and the processes behind it, she discovered that David Driskell was doing a show called *Masters of Print* in Atlanta in partnership with Faith Ringgold. A friend advised her that this would probably be the only time to purchase an affordable David Driskell print. After discovering that you could put art on a payment plan, she decided to make her second major investment. From that point on, she would grab prints if she loved something at a show and even go on studio visits (with some spending money if she could afford it) to purchase pieces from the artist on the spot. From there, her collection grew exponentially.

The *Chambliss Collection* is a series of emerging and mid-career artists from the Atlanta area and a few pieces from artists in Philadelphia and Milwaukee. But, for the most part, Natassha tries to limit her collection to active artists currently around her. The collection is rather eclectic, with over 75 percent of it being print work.

Mrs. Chambliss makes most of her own acquisition decisions, but as more and more money becomes involved, Mr. Chambliss steps in. The very first piece in Natassha's collection, a woodblock by Jamaal, was $300. The last piece she purchased was from Charly Palmer, a Milwaukee-based artist who did a cover for *Time* magazine and the most recent John Legend album cover. The piece was $7,500—probably at a friendly discount, as Natassha personally knows the artist. On an average income, spending $7,500 on a piece can seem excessive, but her husband is generally supportive.

The Atlanta Printmaker Studio is a small studio space inside the Met that has operated for about fifteen years, and they support three artists in residence every year. That carries a lot of meaning for Natassha, who volunteered there for a few years. The studio consists of a series of garage spaces that have been turned into the Mint Gallery. Many artists have spaces there due to the large doors, making it easy to transport equipment. The Printmaker Studio also has printmaking exhibits and facilitates shows in partnership with other galleries, not just locally but internationally as well.

After volunteering for two and a half years, Natassha assumed the board chair of APS. This was her means of immersing herself in the art world, and it allowed her to observe how the curator would select the artwork firsthand. Such experience gave her valuable insight into the curating process and the inner workings of a studio, making her a great asset to the board.

Lines Gallery is another passion project for Natassha. She uses it as a means to stay engaged with art while helping her family and friends. Once in a while, she hosts pop-up events. Last year, she did a fundraiser for Maurice and Grace Evans. Lines Gallery produced a show called the *Nu Africans*, they wanted to craft a coffee-table book with the pieces, so she organized a fundraiser that raised about $10,000 for the cause.

Currently looking for a physical space, Natassha hopes to continue sharing artists' work as a collector. Her goal is to have a permanent revolving exhibit that will include works from the house or road works from her private collection. She has been fortunate enough to sell the work of artists who have trusted her with their pieces online at linesgallery.com.

As someone genuinely interested in investing in the arts, you need a discerning eye to see something unique or extraordinary in artists who will pursue and sustain a long-lasting career. Throughout her journey as a collector, Natassha has become more discerning. Rather than purchasing purely based on aesthetics, she searches for authenticity and craftsmanship, asking herself, "What is this artist doing really well? What is it about their practice that is unique and different and that I would want the world to know about?" She has incorporated these questions into her process of collecting and learned that the more you see, the more you understand, and the more you can ask questions in front of an artist.

Chapter 9

In Support of Young Black Artists

Bernard Lumpkin—Collector, Patron, and the Mind behind Young Gifted and Black

Early in his life as a collector, Bernard Lumpkin extended himself far in every direction, choosing not to limit his efforts in any way. That was how he taught himself the techniques and strategies that would serve him for the rest of his life. All the while he was selecting artworks for his collection, he sharpened his eye, getting a better feel for what he appreciated and how he would make decisions about individual pieces. In 2010, though, his collecting underwent a significant transformation.

It was not one event but a series that shifted Bernard's thinking. After his father received a cancer diagnosis, Bernard took time off from work. He spent all his time with his father that year, listening to stories about what it meant to grow up Black in America. Eye-opening for

Bernard, those stories inspired him to take a closer look at his African American identity, how he would present himself to people, and what both his privilege as a mixed-race person (his mother was Sephardic Jewish, born and raised in morocco) and his heritage as a Black man would signify from then on.

When Bernard's father passed away, the shift in his thinking permeated his art collection. What had been, in his words, a "beginner's collection" soon morphed into a collection intended to raise and highlight African American voices. Laying his father to rest, he considered the possibilities of his collection as a tool for keeping the conversation going—of delving even deeper into himself.

Around the same time, Bernard took a more expansive role in the art world. He had been, until then, a collector and a collector only. Because of the connections that he was seeing between himself and Black artists, he felt an urge to take on more responsibility. Instead of just collecting pieces, he would serve as a patron as well. He would continue to collect art, but he would do more than that. His mission became bigger, emphasizing his ability to support artists and use his position to educate others.

Thinking of himself as a patron, Bernard started to reach out to museums and other institutions. His collection was no longer just his collection but a piece of a wider-reaching journey. Through art, he would teach people about the very things about which his father had educated him. His father, a man who had grown up dreaming of attending Columbia University and becoming a physicist, would keep speaking through the art.

Reflecting on his role as a patron, Bernard points out that he has chosen to work with artists he believed he could impact. He zeroed in on young Black artists. Although he was still acquiring their works, he made introductions to curators, referred them to other collectors, and made himself available for guidance and conversation. However, none of those things is the thing he believes most critical to developing and encouraging emerging talents.

As Bernard puts it, "Art history is not written on my wall; it's written on museum walls. So in order to support an artist's career in a meaningful long-term way, you Must be willing to share your collection with the public. THIS can take many forms. I did it through the "Young, Gifted, and Black" book and exhibition. I also do it by supporting curators, museums, and other arts organizations. this kind of engagement is central to the ethos of what it means to be a patron and not just a collector. A collector keeps; a patron shares. A collector is private; a patron is public."

Bernard explains that, more than anything, it is the effort he puts into spreading artists that has helped them. Toward that end, he has collaborated with the Studio Museum in Harlem by serving on their Acquisition Committee As well as on their board of trustees. he is also a trustee of the Skowhegan school of painting and sculpture. additionally, he serves on the painting and sculpture committee at the Whitney Museum of American Art, and the media and performance committee at the museum of modern art. "i always encourage new collectors to get involved with the museums in their communities; it's the best way to support the artists you love, and it will make you a better collector."

Another event that effected a deep change in Bernard's life collecting began with an exhibition at Concordia College in Westchester in 2019. Engaging with Elizabeth Vranka, the executive director of the Osilas gallery on campus, he spotted an opportunity to push himself, as he had when he pivoted his collection to African American voices. His collection would be able to fill the gallery because it was not overly large, and just as importantly, he would be able to get his collection out into the world even more freely, to connect with the community, and to talk about what the art had come to mean to him.

The exhibition, entitled *Young Gifted and Black*, soon made its way to a second venue, this time at Lehman College in the Bronx. Distributed Art Publishers (DAP) also contacted Bernard, expressing an interest in publishing a book about the exhibition. It would be different from most books about exhibitions: instead of a catalog, the book would create a record of the exhibition, talking about Bernard as a collector, his experience, and his mission. As he says, "It would be a history somewhat of Black patrons. That sort of story hadn't been told in a sort of contemporary comprehensive way ... I really wanted the focus to be the artists: A book by, for, and about artists. So for example when it came to the short texts included in the plates section of the book, we let the featured artists choose whether they wanted to write about their own work, or if they preferred to have a curator write something. This yielded a fascinating set of responses. Jonathan Lyndon Chase submitted a poem. Kevin Beasley took a conceptual approach and asked us to leave one of his allotted pages intentionally blank."

Other artists talked about an exceptional and rewarding experience for a curator to write a book about their work. It was also a singular opportunity for Bernard to call back on all the connections he had made and leveraged up to that point, all the people there for him when he was only starting with his mission. He even asked multiple other curators to contribute to the book themselves. As he describes it, the book was "a gathering of voices, a conversation, a conversation between me and these artists that I've had the pleasure of being in dialogue with over the years; a conversation among the artists themselves in terms of their work and their position as sort of emerging artists in a certain field, whether painting sculpture, photography, or video performance; and then also a conversation between curators and scholars and critics about what is the significance of this group of artists, and the subtitle of the book is a new generation of artists."

The book Has, in turn, been a bestseller, now in its third printing. more importantly, Bernard relates how the book has also become an educational tool to complement the *Young Gifted and Black* travelling exhibition. He says that some of his peers have told him that it acts as a guidebook for curators and collectors looking to champion social justice in the art world. Further explaining the value of the book, he says, "What these artists are doing through their work is providing alternative images of Black bodies, Black joy, of Black lives. They're providing an alternative to the narrow vision of the black experience often found in the popular media. but now people are demanding A new and different vision of blackness, and they're turning to these artists for answers. So when Jennifer Packer paints the Black body, when Jacoby Satterwhite performs desire and eroticism, when Paul Sepuya turns his lens on his friends he's revealing a new vision of Black life. These artists are saying to the world, 'This is who we are. We are not who you see on TV. We are not just that.'"

Noting that the exhibition ran at Lehman College for two weeks before the pandemic lockdowns began, Bernard explains that the book itself had been in production since before the murder of George Floyd. He calls it his "pandemic project," and in that sense, it has been therapeutic for him in that it kept him connected to, and engaged with, his art community. the book will no doubt be similarly therapeutic for the budding collectors and curators who will read it and glean inspiration and knowledge from it.

The *Young Gifted and Black* exhibition, making two stops on the initial leg of its trip from Westchester to the Bronx, has resumed its travels as well, scheduled to appear at the University of Illinois at Chicago; Lehigh University in Bethlehem, Pennsylvania; the University of California at Davis; and the University of Denver.

Vividly passionate about the exhibition, Bernard nonetheless emphasizes the innate value of the book. His view is that the book—which he points out is decidedly "not a money-making endeavor"—is one more means to help artists, as he has been doing in other ways all along. the book was also a learning experience for him. While he was writing it, he explains, he learned other things that he had not known, like the care and attention artists give to the way their work is reproduced. "Doing the book," Bernard explains, "taught me how important it is to keep in mind how an artist's work lives in the world, not just in your home."

These are challenging tasks, the purview of a patron, but Bernard speaks of them with pride, saying, "There's more work, these are things as a collector, as a patron. If you just buy art, you get all the fun with none of the work." In the challenge, in the vigor, in the equity, in the impact, this is how Bernard has chosen to live through art, discovering and bearing himself as a collector and patron.

ELLIOT PERRY—SPORTSMAN, ART COLLECTOR, MEMPHIS COMMUNITY LEADER

A former NBA player, Elliot Perry spent more than a decade in the NBA playing for the Memphis Grizzlies, the Milwaukee Bucks, the Orlando Magic, and the Phoenix Suns. Since the end of his career, he has established himself as a driving force in the art world. Alongside his wife, Kimberly Perry, he has collected many pieces of art, focusing on African American and African artists. His perspective on art collecting and art in general, cultivated over the last two and a half decades, is rich and informative—as is his belief in the power of supporting up-and-coming artists.

Speaking of his entry into art collecting, Elliot recalls a trip he made to Japan in 1996 to play in a series of exhibition games. He was traveling with Darrell Walker, a coach at the time, and Darrell described his forays into art collecting, talking about artists and art theories—topics that were mostly unknown to Elliot then. As he puts it, "I didn't really know anything about art, and so it was just interesting conversation on that long ride."

But what started as a casual conversation soon turned into much more. Elliot and Darrell stayed in touch over the following season. Wherever Elliot was playing, Darrell would direct him to the top art spots: John Wilson's studio in Boston and Bill Hodges's gallery in New York. All the while, Darrell was sending Elliot catalogues and introducing him to standouts and luminaries, as well as offering his insights into art collecting.

Elliot began gradually immersing himself in the shows and exhibitions without purchasing anything. He devoted himself to learning, educating himself about art, studying the pieces that he saw, and picking up tips and guidance along the way. The following year, he purchased his first piece. Then he bought another print—and then a drawing after that. He had begun his art-collecting journey in earnest, deciding that, if collecting was going to become one of his driving passions, he was going to pursue it at the highest levels, assembling the best pieces and the most influential artists possible.

As he explained, he was already thinking about concepts like legacy and posterity. He was looking decades into the future, considering what his collection would mean if he kept up with it for forty or fifty years. His view of this approach is straightforward. "I wanted to try to collect some of the best examples of African-American artists' works, particularly a lot of old-school old masters' works."

Acknowledging what Darrell meant to him when he was starting as an art collector, Elliot also recognizes the importance of access as well as his above-average resources as a professional basketball player. He says that his curiosity and patience played a significant role in his development as a collector as well. Because he was patient enough to learn about art and artists and because he listened to stories about early artists and other collectors, he acquired a wealth of information that he could then apply to the choices he was making. Citing artist Benny Andrews and sculptor Elizabeth Catlett, he emphasizes the importance of conversation—listening, seeking, and accepting.

In the same vein, Darrell also mentions John Wilson, whose studio he visited to spend time around the art and absorbing the history, movement, and talent around him. Darrell also says that the books he read were illuminating for him, and constituted a large part of his enthusiastic study of art. He describes reading one book of particular importance: "I still have my copy, so many red marks, and in-pin marks in the book, just kind of outlining what I was doing . . . What I was doing mostly was, as I read through those books, the things that jumped out at me, those were some of the things I either outline and have on the side . . . Because I felt like those things were something that kind of fed me and those things were something that I needed to really focus on as I go through this journey. And the reason I say that is in order to not to be like, hey, I'm just collecting willy-nilly . . . I do some research of the artists that I wanted to collect, I wrote down some of the names I wanted to collect, and if I was presented with a work, I knew that I wanted to make that move."

In this way, Elliot never went into any galleries or studios blind. He would walk in confident about what he wanted and informed about what was out there, sifting through the art that he came across with a discerning eye and a sharp sense about him. Similarly, he talks about attending shows such as the *Black Art Fair* in New York, the annual *Polk Show*, and *Art Basel* and developing relationships with gallery owners, always finding ways to expand his knowledge and understanding of his pursuit.

Over time, Elliot transitioned from collecting older artists and recognized masters to collecting younger, living artists. In explaining the thought process that led to this transition, he cites Dr. Walter Evans, who described a three-pronged approach to collecting art and making it a force for good: "Supporting the artists early, building relationships with the artists, and lastly, collecting the work." Reading Dr. Evans's words, it was as if he had found a second calling in the art world to not only collect but to empower emerging artists.

Elliot says, "I can support artists early before anybody validates the artists and anybody knows the artists. I can do the same research that I've done with old-school artists and do that with living young, contemporary emerging artists. I definitely can build the relationship with those artists. And then, lastly, I want to collect work, and so that's been important to me, because the one thing that Dr. Walter Evans told me that was the most exciting and that has been the most important thing in his whole journey was the relationships."

Elliot describes his mission in sweeping terms: "We're trying to build a broad collection that encompasses a lot of things about artists. And so, where we love figurative work, we want to make sure that we're supporting abstract artists, African American abstract artists in this mission, minimalist work." Because of his decades-long commitment to art collecting, though, even this sweeping mission seems reasonable. He has put in the time and developed the eye to make a real and immediate difference for emerging artists, becoming adept at spotting talent and vision—as well as the artists who are of interest to him personally.

Today, Elliot says that he collects art using a natural, organic strategy. "We try to collect the best example of that artist's work early." He also sets financial parameters on his decisions, deciding on a range that he wants to operate within and placing his mission within the context of the discussions that he has with young artists. "Before I collect any artist's or any young artist's work, I always have the conversation with them about the mission of our connection." He makes it clear to young artists that he and his wife are not art flippers and that they are collecting art because it means something to them: "We want to build something that is significant as it relates to artists of color."

Talking about representation on boards and at museums, Elliot says that he has seen some change, including increases in African American curators and shows and greater interest in African American artwork for permanent collections at museums. While he notes that this change may not have extended into boards as much as it has into showrooms, he highlights multiple people—AC Hudgins, Pam Joyner, and Ray McGuire—who he believes could make a meaningful and instantaneous impact if they were to become board members themselves, because, "they have not only been the catalyst for more board participation among Blacks (African Americans), but they have done a tremendous job recruiting more African Americans to be board members."

Elliot's passion for art is evident, but as much as he is an art collector, he is also a community leader. He expresses a deep commitment to Memphis, where he sat on the local museum board in the past and where he continues to foster artistic talent and art awareness. For his collection, his long-term plans are clear: "That's been my interest: These works, they go in a museum, where they should be hanging permanently. And that's the reason why we want to collect the best work, so that these works can be out all the time, so that when museum viewers go to the museum, particularly African American people, they see work that attracts them or that looks like them." He seems optimistic about his efforts, saying that he has seen more athletes and entrepreneurs start art-collecting journeys of their own. "This is a rich journey," he says.

LARRY OSSEI-MENSAH—SELF-TAUGHT DISCOVERER OF TALENT

Growing up in the Bronx, Larry Ossei-Mensah's first encounter with visual art was in the form of graffiti that was prevalent in his neighborhood. He practiced tagging in his notebook, subconsciously mimicking the styles he saw. As Ossei-Mensah scanned the pages of magazines like *XXL* and *Source*, he held onto the images that impressed him most. He would spot a provocative photograph and know that it was something that spoke to him, something that he respected. Little by little, he understood what it meant to see the artist's perspective, as he taught himself about technique, style, and the power of cultural expression.

During his junior year of high school, Ossei-Mensah took an internship at Sony Music. He worked in various departments, from promotions to A & R at Epic and Columbia Records until he graduated college. During that time, he started collecting posters of album artwork. It was through these posters that he began to understand the power of image making. Ossei-Mensah went on to graduate school to get his MBA in Switzerland, at Les Roches often traveling on the weekends to London to spend time with his family or to Paris to be with his friends. Along the way, he was immersing himself in the local museums—he had a revelation.

In Florence, at the Uffizi Gallery, he saw sculptures in the Blackamoor style for the first time. Seeing these sculptures opened him up to art a whole-new way of viewing the Black body within an institutional environment. In his own words, "I thought, who were these Black people? They felt familiar, but foreign at the same time. As I pondered the question, I began to realize there has been a significant presence of Black people throughout Europe's history. Saint Maurice was a Black Saint, and so was Saint

Bernard. These are facts that I wasn't aware of at the time. I began to wonder, when was the last time you heard somebody anointing a Black person to sainthood? These facts sparked my investigation around what's the true story. How were Black people present not only in Europe, but in art history? You see these paintings. I always think about the Velasquez's painting of his assistant, Juan de Pareja. He was a brother that not only was an assistant but was also making paintings that may not have always been attributed to him. And so, I just started that journey of questioning everything."

While living in Europe and embarking on this journey of gaining a better understanding of the role of Black people he came across photography as a pathway toward telling his story and insert his POV into the canonical discourse. Larry was diligent in developing his craft with regards to photography for a while. He was making money as a photographer selling some of his artwork. It dawned on him that was not what he was going to do for the rest of his life. He saw his destiny elsewhere, although he was not sure where yet. Through his work in the record industry and his journeys in the art world, he had built a robust network. Although his yearning to be a record man in the music business had waned, he realized that he could do precisely what he wanted to do in the record industry in the art world: discovering talent.

Describing his early experiences with *Art* Basel, Larry talks about doing what most young people were doing: He would put on something *fly* and try to get into the best party possible, crashing at a youth hostel at the end of the night. He was, time and again, just looking for an "in" somewhere. All of that was to change in 2013 when he realized that he could create an 'in' of his own. Along with his collaborator Amani Olu, he put together *Cocktails* and *Curator,* a series of cocktail parties designed to celebrate iconic curators. Hosting events the celebrated curators like Klaus Biesenbach and Franklin Sirmans featuring illustrious co-hosts such as Spike Jonze, Diana Picasso and Dapper Dan opened up a pathway of possibilities for Ossei-Mensah. As he puts it, "We had the 'who's who' in the room and were beginning to realize that the true opportunities sometimes lie in asking, 'What are you offering back to the community?' So, whether it's a party, a dinner, or a brunch, it's in trying to be more proactive in the experience and give back as opposed to just taking."

Art Basel in 2018 and 2019 Larry has curated exhibitions and organized brunches that he has used to build a creative rapport with emerging artists, including Farley Aguilar of Miami, Gisela McDaniel of Detroit, Genevieve Gaignard of Los Angeles to name a few. He has also made a point of staying in Little Haiti rather than South Beach and eating at local restaurants like Naomi's in order to immerse himself in the local flavor that made Miami unique. He emphasizes that all of this helps the community—providing value and making a positive impact.

Talking more generally about his role in the art world and the voice that he has developed, he says that he stays in art more because of the people than the art itself. He describes a lesson that his mentor Bob Buck, who ran the Brooklyn Museum for over a decade, taught him:

Separate what is important from what you like. This is a persistent compromise that he makes. He will thus put art into shows even if the art might not align with his personal taste, but with an awareness that this piece or artistic voice will serve as a creative ballistic for a robust dialogue within the framework of the exhibition. All of this connects to the self-perpetuating ecosystem Ossei-Mensah is working to foster..

In 2009, Larry expanded his role in the art world even further and began collecting art. He recalls that one of his first pieces was by Letha Wilson that he bought from Helen Toomer, a friend who was running a gallery in Chinatown at the time. He cites Nina Chanel Abney as a significant influence on his development as a collector, saying that she encouraged him to take a more aggressive stance while also being fastidious about the quality of the work he was acquiring. Keith Rivers, as well, has helped guide him, while Elliot Perry taught him to stick to his budget for the most part—but to find a way to go past it if the artwork speaks loudly enough. "Keith Rivers talks about art collecting as a means of self-discovery, but he uses no general terms. His descriptions of art collecting clearly define the pursuit as a personal one, and he refers to his father, not knowing a lot about Black history, but 'learning more about my Blackness' in a single breath. Art, to Rivers, is all-encompassing," I said in *The Black Market*.

While he has been collecting, Larry has also continued to learn the ins and outs of the trade on his own. He emphasizes how important it is to keep records of purchases, especially for insurance purposes. He often meets new artists through connections with the artists he already knows and, when he does discover artists, he goes back to the same principle that worked so well for him at *Art Basel*: finding ways to provide value to others. "So, if there's an artist that I believe has talent, I always make sure that other people who may be interested can participate. Again, work early or introduce them to a dealer or a gallerist. So, always make sure you pay it forward. Because then that keeps the deal flowing for you, and you'll always be top of mind because you put collector 'X' on to artist 'Y' when it was $3,000; now it's $50,000."

Cobuying has also been a fruitful approach for him. This has made it possible for him to take on works that he would not have done otherwise by combining his budget with that of someone he trusts and who shares his tastes and values.

When he turns his attention to promoting culture, Larry is expansive. He says that he doesn't believe that Black means to be marginalized or ostracized in all types of art—there can be power in it, and the internet has the capacity to make the movement more impactful. He draws a connection even to literature, finding insights of equal depth in African poetry and Indian and Brazilian writers in places outside the European canon.

In 2018, Larry met David Binder, the Artistic Director of the Brooklyn Academy of Music through his friend and colleague Holly Shen. That led to an opportunity: Larry would serve as the guest curator for the Rudin Family Gallery. After doing an exhibition with Glenn Kaino - *When A Pot Finds Its Purpose* in 2019, the

COVID-19 lockdowns halted all of the other exhibitions he had planned. He remains with the Brooklyn Academy of Music as Curator-At -Large working and is looking forward to organizing exciting exhibition in the gallery and continuing to leverage BAM's digital billboard on Flatbush as forums for discuss as he did with the NY Times heralded 2021's "Let Freedom Ring: A Celebration of Dr. Martin Luther King's Legacy."

Serving on boards and committees himself, Larry highlights the importance of Black representation in power positions because power allows for decision-making. He emphasizes that when there is only one Black voice in a boardroom or a committee meeting, one voice has to stand up alone, making it difficult to push back on injustices and hold people in positions of power accountable. To that point, he drives home how critical it has been for him to witness for himself the internal machinations in places of power. His advice to those looking to do the same is to find a museum to call home, get a museum membership (at trustee level if possible), and fully pursue the mission and vision of that museum.

As a collector, Larry comes back again and again to his love for the work, a love so necessary to recognize and grasp its contribution to history. "Understand the artists; understand the ethos and the mission of the institution. Be proactive." In the process, it's essential to ask questions whenever there is anything opaque or confusing. As a self-taught curator, he has become adept in knowing when to ask a question, thereby detecting his place in the art world, bootstrapping his resources, and developing a curator-collector-benefactor role that's entirely his own.

James Whitner—Changing the Ecosystem through Art

As an art lover who stumbled into the world of collecting in 2013, James Whitner—who doesn't see himself as a collector despite his ever-expanding treasures—sees art collecting as more than just the accumulation of artworks. His curation of space with the art that fits into it is intentional. In addition to the rooms he curates in his home, he spends his professional life curating the spaces he oversees as the owner of The Whitaker Group, a conglomerate of luxury streetwear stores that has expanded into social projects and relief work and may soon be taking on the hospitality business, with one hotel open already.

In contrast to most art collectors, James Whitner didn't grow up in a world surrounded by art. None of the influences around him appeared to appreciate artistic expression, either, and he doesn't recall ever being taken to art museum galleries as a child. Instead, his first steps into the art world in the early days of his retail ventures, where he began to curate the aesthetic of the stores he oversaw. In the process, he learned the value of art, especially when working with local artists to improve the space—and getting to appreciate the importance of local emerging artists. Consequently, in a couple of young stores in Pittsburgh, James and his team created an "Artistic Expression" event where an artist would come into the store, curate the space, and host the show.

He began purchasing art in 2013, when he bought

four KAWS sculptures from the Hakka Foundation through an Asian auction. To this day, they're the only pieces he's acquired from auctions, having a much greater inclination toward galleries. At this time—the very start of his collecting journey—having no mentor and no one around him who collected or had a passion for art. So, he purchased artworks based on his intuition and connection to the pieces; buying pieces that resonated with what he wanted "his existence to feel like." While pondering this first purchase, he called up a friend and asked whether he should bid on four or six KAWS sculptures. Since each sculpture was going for $30,000 at the time, James felt he needed an outside perspective on the investment. Heeding his friend's advice, he ended up buying four of the sculptures. Now, he considers it one of the worst mistakes he's ever made. Since then, he's been more scrupulous in following his volition when buying artworks, focusing on the meaning that they have to him rather than purely receiving a return on investment.

James attributes these first purchases to the influence of street culture; he has been intensely involved with luxury streetwear throughout his professional life. While KAWS already had a big name back then, James recalls that he wasn't as huge a deal as he is today, assessing that it was "the right time" to buy those sculptures. Additionally, continuing down the route of what he considers "street art," acquiring works by Eric Parker, Peter Saul, and Todd James in his early collection. After this, he caught the collecting bug—although he still has a hard time labelling himself as a collector. At first, he focused on saving up for what he describes as "North Star artists," but quickly realized that he preferred to collect works that were uniquely meaningful to him, especially from artists who he discovered for himself. He admits that he "wants to support somebody in the beginning, and help push them up," recalling a piece by Anna Parks that he purchased for about $700, which he now estimates—based on similar works by Parks at auctions—would be worth upward of $40,000.

By comparison, acquiring a Basquiat, is not accomplishing anything—it would be an egotistical purchase for the sake of having a Basquiat and hearing people say: "He's there already." James finds more value in purchasing artworks from rising stars and undiscovered talent whose voices he can help amplify by giving them an ally who patronizes them and their movement.

Now, after almost a decade of collecting, he found himself in the position of being a mentor or advisor to those around him, attributing this to the fact that "everybody around me is now buying art in some way, shape, form or fashion." Because of the rise in art collecting, many collectors have also assumed the role of advisor. His advice to other collectors is unique to each individual, depending on their taste and goals. James advises his friend, for example, to follow his recently discovered love of art and passions for the idea of investing in—and helping to develop—young artists.

The transition from collecting the street-style art with which he had an affinity at the beginning of his journey to buying the kinds of artwork he now possesses happened when he started living in his space and curating his own home. James describes the curation of the areas within his family as intentional; whole parts of his house don't show any artworks, but there is art in the design and texture of the floors, the walls, and even the windows, reflecting the material mix within the space. However, many of his walls are decorated with artworks. When naming the artists that adorn his walls, he lists Todd James, Erik Parker, Nina Chanel Abney, Tomoe Yokoi, and George Condo, among many other exciting contemporary artists.

In twenty years, James admits that he could see his collection gaining significance as a historical marker that people could use to have a sense of the times—for example, art created during the pandemic or influenced by the current racial revolution taking place worldwide. By collecting artists whose works express their response to these tumultuous times, he hopes to amass a body of work that defines the unique sociocultural climate of our day.

At the same time, when asked if he would like to be a part of curating his collection within a museum, James admits he'd prefer someone else to take the reins. James says that in due course, he may like to see his collection exhibited as a show or in a gallery, but only if someone approaches him with the desire to show the work rather than him initiating it.

Now, in contrast to his early days as a lone collector, James Whitner is surrounded by those he considers casual mentors and advisors. These are the people he aims to bounce ideas off and share his passion with. These people are mostly artists themselves, whom he sees as the best advisors: "Once they know you—they can understand what you like and what kind of pieces connect to you after learning what pieces you gravitate towards." Having met most of the artists he knows at galleries, there's ample opportunity for James to make this kind of connection; otherwise, he tends to meet them through other artist friends.

So when it comes to his relationships with the artists, he expresses disdain for the typical "buyer-seller relationship." Instead, he values personal, meaningful relationships with the artists he purchases from—he doesn't want just to be considered another business client. If he feels that he's being treated that way, he probably won't invest in their artwork. James places value in spending time with creatives who see the world how he identifies with it and relates to it, creating a more extensive network of even more people who see the world through the same lens. He drops the name of a small company in the northwest called Good Fat that is developing ways to validate people who "see the world the right way." He explains that there's no singular avenue, as the company focuses on art, community, and a host of other things, putting integrity and a solid moral compass at the heart of the enterprise.

Similarly, James Whitner finds it hard to see himself as a "singular collector of anything," explaining that it's "much broader than that because we live on Earth." Elaborating on this thought, James admits that he "would love to curate an entire city," combining his appreciation for art with his passion for community development. As a real estate investor, he has been thinking about how he can train his focus on developing Black communities and considering how he might "help them value home ownership and help them curate their space." He uses the example of the Detroit City of Murals, recalling how decorating the walls of vacant buildings with murals changed the space and ambiance of the surrounding area, consequently uplifting the community that lived there. This is but one example that illustrates the potential power of art in people's lives.

James describes this world as an ecosystem, underscoring that we need to get more Black people into art to see more Black people in the art industry. He goes one step further and draws a link between underdeveloped communities and the comparatively few Black individuals on the art scene. To change this ecosystem, we need to start by lifting these communities, stipulating that it shouldn't just be the Black community supporting these projects and that White people need to help. "There is real, meaningful change where everyone is involved."

SUZANNE MCFAYDEN—WATCHING ARTISTS EVOLVE AND SUCCEED

Suzanne McFayden has become a noteworthy art collector in recent years. The simplicity of her philosophy, both in terms of her "how" and in terms of her "why," belies the intricacy of her thinking and the sincerity of her passion for what she does.

Of her childhood in Kingston, Jamaica, Suzanne says that her first impressions and lessons about art were deeply patriarchal. She describes the earliest landscapes that she viewed as "very little to do with what was our reality," depicting instead "English countryside and dogs and hunting." These works did little to draw her into art. Still, fortunately, Prime Minister Michael Manley had committed himself to a policy of cultural revival, encouraging a new perspective on Black Jamaican identity. The Prime Minister's efforts gave rise to local art movements.

In those works, Suzanne found material to which she could relate. She saw paintings and sculptures relevant to her day-to-day life, evoking scenes that she could recognize. Another early awakening for her was in family photographs, which she viewed as the most natural and sincere form of art in her life. Contrasting her ideas and experiences with the art that critics and experts seemed to value, she asked herself an important question: "How does this sort of dichotomy happen between what I thought was real art and what I like?"

During her time at Cornell, Suzanne reflected more and dug deeper into this and other questions about her philosophies on art and life. While she had not yet honed in on art as a passion, she did sit for multiple art classes. Practicality was the most critical motivator in college; she focused on legitimate, lucrative jobs that promised money and a living. All the same, the art classes she took a left an impression on her. She realized, once again, that there was a difference between the art to which she could relate and the art that seemed to be part of broader scholarly conversation. She could not help but note one glaring truth in the classes: there were no Black artists included whatsoever.

Living in Geneva, Switzerland, from 2009 to 2011,

Suzanne encountered contemporary art up close. She attended Art Basel, where she was introduced to many of the prominent names in contemporary art. Again, there was the dichotomy, but this time reversed: there, she did see art to which she could relate. One photograph, taken in the Caribbean by Sugimoto, was particularly striking for her. She realized that the artist had visited her hometown in Jamaica, made his art and put his photographs on display for the art world to see and admire.

SUZANNE'S MIND WAS IN MOTION.

At that first trip to Art Basel, she bought a painting by Glen Ligon for approximately 35,000 euros. Afterward, she took something of a respite from art. She had stepped forward as a collector in the thrill of realizing that art could speak to her, but it was only in 2015 and 2016 that she got into collecting again. Talking with an art dealer friend, she decided that she would make another purchase in earnest. This time, she selected a collage work by Wangechi Mutu.

Since then, Suzanne has immersed herself in art collecting. She works closely with Kristy Bryce, whom she calls her collaborator but prefers the title "art advisor." Together, they ask and answer the most pressing questions: "How does each piece acquired shape the collection? What questions does the overall collection ask and answer?"

To Suzanne, these conversations are invaluable. Since the time she graduated from Cornell, having majored in

French Literature, she says that her art taste, knowledge and understanding have matured to the point that she feels confident in her own gaze. Still, she recognizes that in a collaborator (or art advisor), she can tap into insights and knowledge that would otherwise remain peripheral for her. She says that Kristy "has a far deeper trove of knowledge than I do sometimes helps me make better decisions. Also, Kristy is in the market a lot more than I am. I live in Austin, Texas. So even if I come up for free and I go to a lot of art fairs, she's still in the market a lot more than I am."

For example, referring to a show that she attended with Kristy, Suzanne describes asking about an artist, only for Kristy to warn her away because the artist had tended to stagnate over the years. That was a critical note for Suzanne to receive because when she collects an artist, she "wants to stay with them." She talks about collecting artists as a type of relationship, one in which she can stand by as the artists grow, watching them change and evolve, watching them overcome challenges and achieve new triumphs in their work.

Kristy, in Suzanne's view, makes that approach possible. Suzanne talks emphatically about Kristy, portending the success that Amy Sherald achieved after painting Michelle Obama's portrait. "I liked the work. I understood what she was doing, and I thought the work was beautiful," she says. "Then she painted Michelle Obama's portrait, and Amy Sherald could have rested on her laurels. Now Amy has moved forward, and now we're exploring the interior lives of these subjects that weren't in her work before. So that is something that you can get with working with an art advisor in terms of looking at these artists, understanding what they are thinking about, you know, what's their practice, getting to know them. I want a certain rigor in the artists that I'm collecting. I want to know what they're doing, how they're thinking, and an art advisor can help you with that."

Suzanne once called it "a visual expression of how I feel about the world," speaking about her collection. She expands on this thinking by connecting the dots between all aspects of her identity, called "multifaceted." Born into Jamaica, which she says "would be considered a third world country," she cites a list of her core identities: immigrant, Black, woman, mother, divorced. She adds, "I also have had great fortune in my life in the sense that I've been able to have access to places that were growing up as a little girl." She has met the King of Jordan, she has been in the same room as all of the living prime ministers of Israel, and she has bumped elbows and dined alongside global decision-makers and thought leaders.

Despite all of her experiences, Suzanne says that she still connects on a visceral level with one thing that Malcolm X said: "The most neglected person in America is the Black woman." In art—art that speaks to her, not the art that the critics adore, not the skill taught in Ivy League survey courses—she sees herself. This personal identification is, it seems, the crux of her collection and how she interprets its significance in her life.

To Suzanne, it is evident that the act of collecting is immensely personal. She enumerates the things to which she responds in art: pain, unfortunate circumstances, adversity. She also says that she would like to see the artist create beauty out of those darker emotions. She cites Ruth Asawa, a sculptor whose family was torn apart by the Japanese-American Internment when she was a child. The way that Suzanne breaks it down, the pain led, at least to some degree, to novel and interesting stylistic choices, sculptures in which the hurt becomes transcendent. As another example, Suzanne points to Alma Thomas, whose later style was born out of the pain of arthritis, which eroded the large, sweeping strokes that she had favored in her youth—a degradation that yielded beauty as well. Connecting these two, as well as Sheila Hicks and her works often referred to as "domestic arts," Suzanne says that she seeks out artists who are "creating something that brings joy to the page."

More recently, Suzanne has collected Alison Janae Hamilton. The 37-year-old artist first caught Suzanne's eye for equally personal reasons: going through Hamilton's portfolio, Suzanne saw photographs that featured two little girls who reminded Susan of her own two daughters.

Shifting to the more technical side of collecting, Suzanne rattles off a series of concerns about collecting photographs (where to display them), collecting paintings (what to do when shadows pop up because of multiple layers), and collecting brass sculptures (how to clean them). She also says, "Private collectors need to understand that you are going to have to spend money to conserve your collection, and that starts with good storage." She touches again on a litany of issues with storage: UV protection, moisture fluctuations, condition reports, work stability, and systems for collection management, to name a few. Summarizing all of these issues, she says, "If you're going to spend the money to acquire it, you should take care of it."

In September 2021, Suzanne will begin as chair of the Blanton Museum of Art Board at the University of Texas, near Austin. She first involved herself in Blanton in 2015. There, she will be able to make her voice heard, speaking up for the assertively personal philosophy that has defined her collection and helping direct the conversation toward the sort of art that she has always loved and that she continues to pursue.

Chapter 10

The Business of Art

Why Investment in Art?

I bought some artwork for one million/
Two years later, that shit worth two million/
A few years later, that shit worth eight million/
I can't wait to give this shit to my children.
—Jay-Z, "The Story of O.J." (2017)

While the three-time Grammy-nominated track "The Story of O.J."—written and produced by billionaire rapper Jay-Z—illustrates the pervading stereotypes and racism endured by Black people in America, regardless of their status or financial state, the track also alludes to the importance of economic freedom, with the rapper citing art as a lucrative financial investment. Indeed, Jay-Z and wife Beyoncé are enthusiastic patrons of the arts, with names such as Basquiat and Warhol gracing the walls of their home, alongside many other artists of note and value.

Despite this, only a tiny fraction of artworks appreciate

over time, and—no matter what hip-hop icon Jay-Z might have us believe—it's improbable that an artwork you purchase this year will be worth eight times what you paid for it a few years later down the line. However, the art market represents one of the most overlooked asset classes, with a market value of $1.7 trillion, according to estimates by Deloitte, and outperforming the S&P 500 by close to 200 percent.

Likewise, successful investments can be made in the art world for a profitable return and represent a valuable asset. The recent Phillips auction, which took place in December 2020, saw the sale of artworks from some of the most exciting contemporary Black artists, with appreciated values that make "The Story of O.J." lyrics seem a little less far-fetched. A work by Mickalene Thomas, for example, had an estimated value of around $200K and went for over $900K, while a piece by Amy Sherald—estimated at approximately $150K—sold for over $4,250,000.

However, the profits gained from the vast majority of profitable art acquisitions are usually more modest, at least in the grand scheme of things. More routes have become available for art enthusiasts to invest in art, even if they don't have millions to spare in cash, particularly in the online world.

In the last year, as a result of the COVID-19 pandemic and the measures enforced to suppress the virus—including the shutting of galleries, museums, and art studios, in addition to the social distancing measures, which meant that art dealers and buyers were prevented from the meeting—the art market has shrunk by around

22 percent, as reported by the Art Basel and UBS Art Market Report.

Despite this, thanks to the global shift of the art industry to the digital world—like the majority of sectors have during this period—online sales soared to $12.4 billion during 2020, representing an online art market value of double the previous year and estimated to be the highest value of art sales ever made online. Likewise, many budding art collectors and investors have used the enforced isolation that defined much of 2020 to complete online art purchases and take their first steps into online art investment.

One of the pioneers of accessible art investment is the fractional ownership platform Masterworks, launched in 2017 by art collectors and led by founder Scott Lynn. While blue-chip art investment was only accessible to the ultrarich, Masterworks allows investors who believe in the art market's financial potential to buy shares representing a small investment in valuable masterpieces.

The data experts at Masterworks have collected data from over 300,000 auctions, representing over three million data points about art purchases, and use in-house analytics to assess the artist and the momentum the artwork currently has in the art market. While only a tiny fraction of paintings appreciate over time, the masterpieces that Masterworks has physical ownership of are, they say, precisely the kind of artworks that have seen large capital growth over time—the type of artworks that only the ultrawealthy could previously afford and, likewise, financially benefit from the investment in the long run.

While the Masterworks platform focuses on delivering financial rewards from unattainable masterpieces for the many, other similar platforms, such as Art Money, cater more to art collectors—those who want to possess the art, rather than those who simply want to make a financially savvy investment. The Art Money platform allows its members to buy artworks through the platform in rapid time. The venue pays the gallery or dealer upfront for the total value of the painting so that the collector doesn't miss out due to lack of liquidity or insufficient funds. Then, the collector pays the platform back in a series of ten installments over ten months. One of these installments is paid when they request a purchase via the site; the following nine payments are paid back over the next nine months, with no interest, as the galleries who partner with Art Money pay a 10 percent commission to the platform for every sale made. So there's no downside to the collector or art investor, granting access to a slew of artworks that collectors may not have been able to afford comfortably before.

In an interview with a representative from Art Money, the representative admitted to approving "a client for a sale that he would have never been able to access," although they reveal that 90 percent of the clients the platform works with can afford the works they buy through Art Money, they "just choose not to", the rep says. In this way, Art Money relieves some of the massive financial dents that investing in valuable art can make in an art collector's pocket, as ten smaller payments made over ten months is significantly more feasible for many than a one-time sum or installments made over three or four months to a gallery or studio, without the help of Art Money.

So, while Art Money isn't a platform that focuses on investment in terms of the rewards to be had from the appreciation of artworks' value over the years—unlike the art investment platform Masterworks—it does make the opportunity to acquire these appreciative works of art easier to come by. By purchasing artworks through Art Money, collectors are dealt less of an immediate financial blow, which may have discouraged them from making a potentially fruitful art investment.

Another platform whose function is comparable to Masterworks is fractional ownership platform Otis. Otis markets itself as "The Stock Market for Culture," selling shares in collectibles, rare comics, and art, among other cultural relics. The Rally platform too works on an almost identical basis, offering shares in items such as art and collectibles that investors can buy and sell.

While in recent years, the opportunities for art investment have grown, as these online investment platforms' function indicates that it's challenging to have your cake and eat it when it comes to the world of art investment. Purchasing art that's highly likely to appreciate over time is usually not possible for those outside of the ultrawealthy circle of art patrons. Therefore, it is impossible to reap the benefits of their appreciation. However, in recent years several of these online investment platforms have made it possible for every man to make blue-chip art investments alongside numerous others who claim partial financial ownership of the artwork. However, the catch is that—unlike Jay-Z—these investors will never be granted the opportunity to acquire physical ownership of the work and have the chance to see it hanging in their own space. In this instance, whereby an individual is a budding collector—rather than simply an investor—a platform such as Art Money might help collectors outside of the mega wealthy get their foot in the door, allowing them to pay for artworks in manageable installments when they might have previously second-guessed the purchase due to the financial strain of paying upfront, despite the possibility of the artwork appreciating over time.

The final option for art collectors and investors who want to make a few million from the art investment game is to purchase an artwork from an unknown, up-and-coming artist and simply hope that in a few years they'll be an international superstar. However, without a lifetime's worth of luck, you might be better off choosing another more modestly rewarding but more reliable route of art investment.

Understanding Today's Art Market—and Preparing for Its Challenges

In 2019, sales in the art market reached $64.4 billion, a massive figure, but one that seemed poised to continue to increase. Year after year, that was the pattern. However much sales figures increased, it appeared that they would continue to move in that direction. It seemed that there was no limit to the heights to which the market could ascend. No one thought that the flow was going to slow down.

Then, it did. The slow came to a screeching halt, and in 2020, the art market shrank by 22 percent, amounting to just over $50 billion. Economist Dr. Clare McAndrew outlined this and other insights into the downturn that the market experienced in her report "The Market 2021," which Art Basel and UBS made available.

According to Dr. McAndrew, between March 15 and April 15, 2020, gross revenues plummeted 85 percent year over year. That was an unprecedented catastrophe for the market, setting projections back far beyond any lows or even correction marks than anyone would have projected. Galleries, meanwhile, experienced a 31 percent overall decrease in gross revenues throughout the first quarter of 2020. While that figure is undoubtedly less disconcerting than the 85 percent decrease, it is essential to note that a 30 percent decrease equates to a massive amount of revenue over a quarter.

To make matters worse, the second quarter of 2020 led to a 73 percent loss in gross revenue for art galleries in the United States. Throughout New York, gallery owners tried to renegotiate the terms of their leases, doing whatever they could to make ends meet, stretching their budgets as thin as they could, and looking for lifelines anywhere that they could find it. The setback, along with the tragedy that went with it, was wiping out people's savings and rendering them incapable of doing their work. Businesses shuttered.

Few people may realize that businesses experienced no support because of the pause placed on residential evictions. For gallery owners and the artists to whom they cater, there was little in the way of help available— at first. Once PPP loans started to roll out, some galleries could keep their staff on their payrolls, with 85 percent of art-gallery staff holding on to their jobs.

All of this is to say that when disaster struck, it struck everyone. It might have started with the gallery owners, but before long, it had touched artists, art handlers, framers, designers, art shippers, and all of the ancillary business owners who serve the art market in their ways. Finally, it touched the collectors as well.

We can understand this situation best, perhaps, by examining dealer sales. Again, between 2019 and 2020, there was a significant decrease, the figure dropping 20 percent to $29.3 billion. Within these figures, though, we can find an important lesson as well, one that will reverberate for all people in a crisis. We can learn something from the art dealers, considering the circumstances in which they found themselves and, in turn, the results that they drove.

Remembering that dealer sales decreased by 20 percent in 2020, you may be surprised to learn that many dealers managed to eke out a profit by reducing their business costs, more than a quarter of them increasing their earnings from 2019. Their methods were simple and far from revolutionary: they moved their businesses online, the same way that so many other professionals did. Whereas they would have lost almost all of their clients and closed all of their sales in person, they began to leverage online chats and online sales.

To elucidate what art dealers learned when they faced

a crisis, think about what it represents. The most obvious point would be that the future is digital. Anyone who resists e-commerce and remote communications is going to struggle during the years ahead. If we look deeper at what has happened, though, we can find a more general lesson. We can derive a lesson applicable to our own lives, what we are doing as collectors, and how we strategize for the future.

It comes down to flexibility. When the tides turn and outlooks get grim, everyone in the art world needs to be willing to rethink what they have been doing. Toward that end, we all need to learn about the options available to us to pivot as quickly and as efficiently as possible. If circumstances change, we should be able to change with them. We should feel comfortable fundamentally altering our plans and our approaches if conditions demand that we do so. In the art world, there are potential setbacks on the horizon at all times. Whether or not they look like the setbacks we have faced in the past, we need to understand and respond to them.

Others may conclude that there will be safe harbors amid a downturn, environments that go untouched because of their character or status. That may be the case, but to grasp the exceptions, we need to grasp what the crisis is doing to change people's lives. Public auction sales of art, for example, declined by 30 percent between 2019 and 2020. Simultaneously, private sales increased 36 percent. This information is applicable only in retrospect, however. Each crisis will force different trends and adaptations. In another situation, it is believable that the inverse would be true; public sales would increase while private sales would decrease.

Again and again, it is clear that whenever we see shifts, something that indicates an opportunity or a danger, we should take the signal-to-noise ratio with a grain of salt. Instead of jumping to any significant conclusions, instead of painting with thick, broad brushstrokes, we should remember that as crises change, only our knowledge and education will save us. Specific, concrete decisions made in the most recent situation may prove disastrous in crises that happen later.

Research is the solution. The all-covering, all-encompassing tool, research will enable you to stay prepared for any crises. You never need to say definitively what you will do when you encounter the next setback or when the art market starts to seem shaky. Instead, you can feel confident simply because you have put thought and effort into your plans in the most abstract sense. You have been learning, reading up on the market, and understanding how all the pieces fit together.

Art fairs and live events exemplified this reality with exceptional clarity. In 2020, 61 percent of planned art fairs did not take place due to cancellation. A significant minority, however, found another way to move ahead with their plans: 37 percent put together alternative live events, and 2 percent put together hybrid events. A majority planned a virtual form of their events, although there will always be something missing when events are not in person. "Art fairs are the ideal environment for networking. These events provide a place where artists can share their work, where they can teach others about their own progression, and where collectors can make meaningful purchases and glean insights into where the market might be headed," I wrote in *The Black Market*.

The takeaway here is that, like event planners, all other participants in the art market need to be willing and able to change their plans and do something else if the first plan fails in some way. If the piece you have been looking for or the artist you have been scouting becomes unavailable, you need to make a shift. This is the crossroads of flexibility and research: you know what you want, you are willing to change that, you stay up to date on your options, and you learn more and more.

Another less direct lesson from art fairs and live events is that when fewer happened, a substantial number of the highest-net-worth collectors purchased anyway: 41 percent of all collectors, in 2020, shopped at art fairs. That number says something about the assumptions that we tend to make. While most art fairs and live events were shuttering their doors, there were still big-ticket spenders out there, frequenting the art fairs that welcomed them, supporting those who were willing to go against the grain.

It would have been impossible to know that those sales were available, of course, if you were running one of the art fairs or live events that canceled. The same truth applies to collectors and the strategies that we use to find pieces and artists. Unless we are putting ourselves out there, trying every possible avenue, and stretching ourselves beyond the most apparent opportunities, we will wind up missing out on something. We may find some of the things that we want, but we will likely see that we have missed other things we would have liked in retrospect.

The Brilliance of the Color Black | 157

Another shocking statistic that has emerged out of all this is that, according to a survey from Arts Economic and UBS Investor Watch, 66 percent of high-net-worth collectors said that their interest in collecting went up because of the most recent crisis. Many of those collectors were millennials; 30 percent of all high-net-worth millennial collectors spent more than $1 million throughout the year.

For anyone who had looked at only the surface statistics—those describing the closures and the cancellations, those referring to the overall decrease in sales—such an increase in enthusiasm might have seemed impossible. They would have assumed, reasonably enough, that anyone who continued to collect would have done so with more, rather than less, reluctance and hesitation.

The opposite was often true, though. Enthusiasm went up, and, without research, no one would have guessed that. Think about all that this metric means, how it flies in the face of conventional wisdom and so-called "common sense." While the surveys and the numbers are out there, waiting for anyone to read them, you would never have guessed them because you would never have imagined them. You would never have been able to take advantage of the truths that they communicated, either.

This is only one truth among many, too. In the art market, especially when there is a crisis, the savviest collectors are the ones who make an effort to know all of the other collectors better—the ones who invest their time into understanding dealers and the behavior that is going to define most transactions shortly. Setbacks do happen, and when they do, collecting becomes a battle for information. Whoever can know more and say more will be able to do more. The winners will be those who have done their research diligently and sincerely, peering past the run-of-the-mill information and reading between the lines of others' interpretations of market conditions.

Consider the shift toward the digital that has taken the art market by storm over the last year. That was something that many experts and commentators had predicted, and yet until it happened, it seemed that few people were willing to put any capital on their opinions. In the earliest days of this trend, though, research and insight would have afforded any collector an advantage. Seeing the changes taking place, the ones that experts and commentators had already been writing about, a collector could have conceivably taken action more quickly than others in the market.

That is the value of research, in a nutshell. Forget about the specifics. Forget about the time frame. Forget about how and when the crisis took place. All that matters is that it took place and, before long, another one will take place, too. When it does, research will become your go-to tool. You can lean into the research you have done, knowing that you can do additional research if necessary. The collector must seek out and gather information to understand what is going on in the market, stave off the effects of a crisis, and make better decisions about sales and purchases. Today's market conditions demand it, but even in more normal times, research will provide benefits.

ANWARII MUSA—COLLECTOR AND ADVISOR

Born and raised in Queens, New York, Anwarii Musa

got his start at Sotheby's when he was still young, taking on a one-year internship. That was an active learning experience for him. He immersed himself in all of the departments at Sotheby's and engaged in hands-on work such as transporting art and papers throughout the organization. He drew attention from others at Sotheby's for his devotion and passion, and little by little, he built a reputation for himself there. At the end of the internship, he moved into a full-time role, becoming an art handler and learning even more about the industry. Around that time, he began to pick up on the nuances of the business of art.

Up to that point, Anwarii had been seeking a purpose and a direction in his life. He knew that he wanted to go into the arts, and when he entered Sotheby's, it was clear that he was in the right place. He found their approach to art more "grassroots," especially because of an exhibition they did centered around Martin Luther King's collection. It connected with him in a profoundly personal way.

Over the next five years that he remained there, he cultivated relationships both with business leaders and academics. Along the way, he noticed a distinct lack of people of color in the building; aside from celebrities, he saw few others who looked like him. Thinking of ways that he could counteract that and make an immediate impact, he shifted his attention toward advisory roles. In *The Black Market*, Musa stated that it is important for Black collectors to collect Black art. For him, it comes down to Black collectors becoming part of the conversation.

It was a Michael Jordan "casino night"–style

fundraiser that cemented this drive. Anwarii watched as thousands of people walked in and out of the building, and almost everyone that made up a collective sea of faces was White. Eager to contribute to the culture, he also realized that he was earning more money outside of his job than he was during his everyday job because of the network he had built. That was a wake-up call to him, nudging him toward even more ambitious endeavors.

So in 2014, Anwarii launched his advisory firm, ArtMatic, with only ten clients—all of whom he was close to and who have remained clients to the present day. Because this was a boutique firm, he saw immediately how critical it was for him to focus on the relationships and foster them as attentively as possible.

Over the four years that followed, Anawarii's efforts weren't for naught. Self-funding the venture, he spent his savings on an airplane ticket and a hotel for *Art Basel*, doing all he knew how to do to tap into the art scene and to continue to cement the connections that he knew would make all the difference. Sure enough, this paid off. Soon, he had nearly tripled his total clients, from ten to between twenty-five and thirty. He continued to invest in ArtMatic, hiring attorneys, financial analysts, and other support staff, and he even expanded his network by visiting Hong Kong, Switzerland, and London for the first time. All of the knowledge that he had accrued and the understanding that he had developed enabled his advisory firm to expand to more than two hundred clients.

Following that rapid growth, Anwarii still speaks about art in personal and human terms, referring to his business connections as he would refer to a friendship or any other informal relationship. As he puts it, "I think people are taken back because they don't feel they have access to an art advisor. I don't necessarily go straight to art advising when first working with a client, because they would just feel that's somebody that wants to take their money. I think when they have a conversation with me, they realize this guy is not really thinking about the money." He points out that he takes a genuine interest in helping his clients build their collections from scratch, priding himself on his ability to introduce them to new books, artists, galleries, institutions and other insider information on the art industry.

As a professional in the art world, Anwarii seems equally forthright about his knack for picking out trends before they have caught on with the masses. He links this preternatural gift to his experience and education, referring specifically to his early days at Sotheby's. Learning about the industry and the market, he says that he would often encounter artists who would become the next generation of successful artists; and it was only then when he fully appreciated his position and could parlay those encounters into something tangible—an awareness of movements and trends in the market. A piece of advice he would offer is: "When it comes to my clients, I never just tell them about a trend. I always study what they like, and I tell them what they should assess and what they should go after. And then that starts the conversation. The conversation never starts on who's the hottest. It always starts on what's your aesthetic, what do you like."

This advice seems especially incisive coming from

someone like Anwarii, who speaks just as effortlessly about institutional collectors like the Yale Art Gallery, the Princeton University Art Museum, and the Harvard Art Museum buying up the major and emerging artists of the current generation. Of these collectors, he says that there is a distinction between "who's a part of the conversation and who's leading the conversation." He explains that in his earlier years when he worked with institutions, he did not see people of color in positions to make decisions. He goes on to add that the majority of decision-makers were not aware of Black successful artists because up to that time themselves never collected the works of Black artists.

Looking back on his experiences with top collectors, Anwarii explains that once the collectors have realized they have shut themselves out of major movements in the art world, they are often without any immediate recourse. They need to find people who have collected the artists for twenty or thirty years to understand what they are looking at. This is why he recommends that new collectors involve themselves in key institutions through committee memberships and young collectors' committees.

Anwarii believes that a fundamental disconnect in many Black people's minds is thinking about art as an asset. "I think the biggest cliché for Black people is that we don't talk about assets amongst each other. I think when it comes to art, it's even more relevant. Me being on the business side of the art industry, I tell you right now that art should be a part of your asset allocation. There are different levels of collecting art. There's the speculative collectors. The very knowledgeable collectors and then there is the collectors as patrons. And I think when you've reached that peak, that's when you realize it—art is an asset… you have to treat your collection like a full-time business. For example, when collectors give works out as loans to museums, they have to treat that like a business transaction."

In this way, Anwarii interprets and explains the role of an art advisor as being nearly identical to that of a financial advisor or a legal advisor. He gathers his resources and offers his guidance to clients, all to limit the number of mistakes that they might make in the big decisions they undertake. He sees this as a natural progression; it only makes sense for someone to seek information from a professional. In his own words, "You should still think about the art as an investment. Because, if you have a piece in your house, every collector should have their work appraised every ten years, five to ten years, depending on how big your collection is. That right there is a whole process."

Even for artists and studios, Anwarii has sharpened his sense of best practices as such that he can see through the mistakes that they often make in their interactions together. He sees trust as the cornerstone of these interactions, describing how a lack of transparency between the artists and their studios and managers can lead to uncomfortable, unproductive situations. When he is talking about all of this, his thought process as an advisor becomes clearest. He is asking questions from every angle: "Do you trust that gallery? Do you trust that artist's liaison to help you manage it the right way?"

To collectors, Anwarii recommends becoming

familiar with all of the connections available and understanding how artists, studios, and managers are all working together. Make sure that galleries are showing the artists' work to the right people, like curators, and placing their work with notable institutions. This is all the more for collectors to grasp what they are buying and how they are making their choices at one gallery or another. He connects back to his concept of "real collectors," those who are thinking about their collection as a business and treating their pieces as assets.

To understand how this concept has remained so elusive in the Black community, Anwarii looks back to the history of America, "and while working at Sotheby's understanding since the London company first established in 1744, it took over 200 years for Blacks to be part of the conversation of having assets to trade in America and throughout the world. To think about that, knowing that fifteen percent of America is Black. When we first got to this land as workers, what we did was worth billions and even trillions in modern-day history. The wealth gap started there but I strongly feel art can play a vital role in changing that gap."

To Anwarii, though, the crux of the conversation is whether or not Black collectors and Black artists can break into the institutions, where he sees the most critical aspects of the art world taking root. He emphasizes the value of ownership, saying that, even while he was working at one of the largest companies in the world, he was perpetually looking for ways that he could create and own something of his own. That is how he is making an outsized impact in the art world.

Lola C. West—Five-Decade Art Collector and Accomplished Wealth Manager

Co-Founder and Managing Director at Westfuller Advisors, Lola C. West also serves on the Board of Directors for Souls Grown. Deep Foundation.

Souls Grown Deep advocates the inclusion of Black artists from the South in the canon of American art history and fosters economic empowerment, racial and social justice, and educational advancement in the communities that gave rise to these artists. Souls Grown Deep derives its name from a 1921 poem by Langston Hughes (1902-67) titled The Negro Speaks of Rivers, the last line of which is "My soul has grown deep like the rivers."

Souls Grown Deep Community Partnership pursues racial, social, and economic justice by grant-making, values-aligned investments, underwriting projects, advocacy, and forging collaborations with a variety of like-minded civic organizations, businesses, and nonprofits.)

Tracing her collecting back to a Norman Lewis show, Lola recalls an early piece of advice that her friend and expert in Black art... Peg Alston, who curated the show, offered to her: "Buy art that you love, because you have to look at it every day. Don't buy for an investment. Buy because you love it." She took that advice wholeheartedly, deciding that unless she had fallen in love with a piece, she was not going to buy it. At the show, she came across an acrylic that jumped out at her—and she immediately made it her own.

Sometime after, Lola attended another of Peg's shows, this time for Lubaina Himid. She bought another piece, too, something that had become normal for her by then, and thirty-odd years later, Lubaina Himid won The Turner Prize. At the time, she had simply found something that caught her eye: a large portrait of Frederick Douglass and another smaller piece. As it happened, it was fortunate that the Frederick Douglass piece had caught her eye when it did—another woman came along not long after eager to buy the same piece, having watched it throughout the show but saying nothing to anyone.

That is Lola's personality as an art collector. She sees a piece that she wants and then acts, swiftly reaching out and obtaining it. Telling another story—this one about Norman Francis, the longtime president of Xavier University—she highlights how action mixed with serendipity has defined her art experiences so often. Visiting the Francises during the Essence Music Festival, she came across an Elizabeth Catlett drawing along with some prints. Specifically, prints that both Catlett and Stevie Wonder had signed. In Dr. Francis'own words, "Stevie loved it so much and wanted to help us with a fundraiser that he signed it and she signed it." So, I said, 'You got any left?' And he had one left. I said, 'I'll buy it.' I bought it and I have that."

Lola goes on to emphasize, "Everything I have, I love." She says that her passion for art extends to her childhood. When she was in middle school, a Black art teacher became a mentor to her, encouraging her in her work throughout the seventh, eighth, and ninth grades. She ended up in the honors art program at her high school in Brooklyn. There, her neighborhood was almost entirely white, and in her honors classes, there were no Black children. On the first day of her high school art class, her teacher told her to draw something, anything, and when she did, he said, "You call that art?"

Although that moment discouraged her within the context of the class, the art lover inside of her remained strong. She found herself attracted to photography and drawing as well as some design work, working hand in hand with the designer she hired to do her home.

Traveling around the world, Lola has let the art lover inside her breakout fully and utterly, making a point of visiting anywhere that she can find arts and crafts. During one stop in South Africa, she met a vendor who was ostensibly creating and selling key chains but realizing that they were much too large to fit inside a pocket or to function as a key chain of any kind, she repurposed them into accents for her cabinets and doors by removing all her doorknobs and putting up the "key chains" in their places.

Describing her strategy for finding art and discovering new artists, Lola talks about the unique position that her career has afforded her. She manages both artists' and collectors' wealth as part of her business. She had made friends throughout the art world previously, so her network now includes many gallery owners and other collectors.

As for the styles that she collects, Lola seems intent on not limiting herself in any way. She includes abstract and figurative works in her collection, leaning only slightly toward the figurative. There are also many photographs in her collection, many of which she purchased in the 1970s before attending the Norman Lewis show and before she started to buy art in galleries. She speaks with enthusiasm about the photographer Emerson. "There was a fair in Brooklyn that happened every year. He sold thousands of pictures when he was there because no one was doing that ... These are all color photographs that this man did that I just like: one of them is a picture of five women ... and he said, 'Lola, do you know where they are?' And I was ... like, no, but I'd like to. He said, 'Lola, they all have their shoes off. They are standing in front of a mausoleum, and they've just come out of it.' It's stunning, and I've carried these women with me and almost every office I was in from the seventies on, and now I keep it in my kitchen."

In this story and the others, she tells, Lola speaks with an enthusiasm that has clearly propelled her through her forty-plus years as a collector. She has set up her home like a salon, lining it with art from one entire wall to the other so that in a single moment, she can sit down inside and look at the bulk of her vast collection from a clear line of sight.

Lola's collection includes luminaries from the 1970s onward: Claude Lawrence, Romare Bearden, Mickalene Thomas, Faith Ringgold, Oliver Johnson, Jason Wallace, Art Bacon, Debra Grant, Chris Ofili, Cheryl Riley, Charles Moore, Lyle Ashton Harris, Nina Chanel Abney, Elizabeth Catlett, Frank Stewart, Derrick Adams, Mary Pettway, Thokozani Mthiyane, Charles Shelton, and Charles White, among others. She says that in the long term, she plans on giving away her collection, although as of now, she has not decided how she will do that.

When Lola talks about her art, even when she talks about appraisals and valuations and appreciations, she soon returns to gushing about the joy that she has found in her pieces. She has bought the pieces that she loved, not the pieces that others told her would make her money. For those who are thinking about their art as an investment, though, she offers pointed advice: "Do your research. If you're going to go out and buy art, figure out how much you want to spend, look at artists who are in your price range, but also allow yourself to be wooed and surprised. But you cannot not like a piece of art and buy it. It just doesn't make any sense. What are you going to do? What are you going to buy it for? Put it behind the sofa? Wait for it to go up in value if you don't like it?"

As a wealth manager, Lola works with many people who are thinking of art as just that, and day to day, she needs to think of art in the same way, viewing it as an asset class. She offers advice to people based on how their art figures into their overall wealth. This is something that she recommends strongly: "It makes all the difference in the world. Because just look at what happened to people who own even a little bit of Black art now. They're in a completely different place. It is an asset class. We believe in art, fine automobiles, yachts, and ships—all of that. People who have money need to divest and diversify." However, at her core, she is undeniably passionate about art for its own sake—a collector and lover who understands art from a multitude of perspectives.

THE ROLE OF THE ART LAW ATTORNEY

As art collectors, we want to be able to focus on the art

side of things—appreciating the artwork we have, finding the best new pieces for our collection, and engaging in philanthropy—rather than being burdened by the legal responsibilities and financial complications that can arise as a by-product of our favored hobby.

As such, the time comes in many collectors' lives when they consider whether or not to seek the counsel of a law attorney, who can be helpful at all stages of ownership, from prepurchase contract negotiations to tax mitigation and legacy planning. As the value of the artworks, you purchase increases—or the value of paintings you own appreciates—so, too, does the importance of consulting an art law attorney.

With this in mind, we interviewed three leading art law attorneys—Megan Noh, Pamela Grutman, and Gabrielle C. Wilson—to gain insight into why art collectors approach them and in what situations they can provide the most value to their clients.

Before art collectors even own artwork, they can benefit from the counsel of an art law attorney, who can help to ensure the transfer of title of the painting they're purchasing and put measures in place to make sure they're protected if the art they buy proves to be inauthentic.

Megan Noh—partner and cochair of art law at Pryor Cashman—asks herself, "What can my clients do before they pay money for something to prevent a problem from happening later?" She advises that several things need to be taken into account to safeguard her clients. While she notes that "if you're acquiring a work by contemporary living artists from their primary representation—from the gallery that represents this artist—then you're probably not going to be concerned about authenticity", Noh says that the gallery should still "warrant that it's authentic". There are laws in place—at least in New York—that ensure that galleries take responsibility for the authenticity. For example, when an art buyer receives an invoice from a gallery—and the invoice states that the buyer has purchased a particular artwork, describing said artwork—they effectively provide a warranty for the work's legitimacy.

However, art collectors should be wary of purchasing artworks on the secondary market. Noh states that, when buying on the secondary market, "even if it's by a contemporary living artist, you want to make sure it's not fake." Sometimes, this can mean ensuring that the artwork has a certificate of authenticity, although in many cases, the artist may not have a practice of certification. In these instances, it might be prudent to verify provenance or to check directly with the artist's studio to get confirmation that the work being sold is legitimate; this is how auction houses typically validate that the artwork they've received is authentic before they allow it to go on sale.

Moreover, with any sale of an artwork, there should be a warranty—a period in which, if the work is shown to be inauthentic, the buyer receives a refund. As a clause of this warranty, the buyer will usually be asked to prove that a work isn't authentic, and this can result in the buyer having to prove this in court. On the other hand, an attorney can help you modify the warranty agreement so that if, for example, a major auction house or museum refuses the work due to concerns about its attribution, it will trigger the purchaser's rescission rights. Noh says that she often "encourages her clients to add alternative dispute resolution provisions into their private contracts so that issues don't automatically end up in public litigation."

The second significant prepurchase consideration is ensuring the transfer of title—i.e., ensuring that the buyer is granted ownership of the artwork. Noh notes that, unlike most other assets, there isn't one universal document to prove that you have right to the painting, such as the deed for a house or the single title document that stays in the car and allows the old owner to sign it over to the new owner. Instead, when it comes to art, Noh states that "sometimes the purchaser will be able to show that they've acquired title just based on the gallery invoice" when it's combined with a record of proof of payment and your bank records that show evidence of the transfer.

At auctions, Noh recommends keeping the auction catalog (as proof that the artwork was on sale), the invoice that you receive after the auction (to show that you were due to pay a certain amount as the winning bidder), and the bank records showing that you sent that amount of money to the auction house (to prove your rightful ownership of the artwork). Noh admits that making purchases from auction houses typically allows you to obtain title more easily. At least in New York City, where Noh practices law, the DCA regulates auctioneers. These auctions are considered a public—rather than a private— place of sale, so the auctioneers are liable to pass you a good title and are "required to have representations and warranties from their consigner" that show the consigner can pass the title over to the purchaser. On the other hand, title disputes can arise with older artworks. Noh gives the example of property coming from the World War II era, whereby claims have been made on property sold in auction houses by heirs of Holocaust victims, who had their property taken from them during the war.

In private sales, Noh advises that there should be a bill of sale, which she says "can be a one-page document saying 'I the seller confirm that, as of X date, I received the funds and the title has passed.'" She further stipulates that "you wouldn't sign that at the same time as a purchase agreement because the purchase agreement shows the parties' commitment to pay on a certain future forward-looking schedule." However, Noh explains that it's a good idea to have a clause of the purchase agreement put the seller under obligation to provide a bill of sale—a piece of paper that her clients can keep on file to show that the title did pass and that the payments were made—after a particular period after the costs have been passed.

However, in circumstances where work has been stolen and subsequently sold, the title may not be transferred to the buyer, as the title of the artwork may not have been the sellers to give away in the first place—whether that's known to them, or not—due to a basic tenet of US property law that a buyer cannot obtain a good title to stolen property. Gabrielle Wilson, associate at Herrick, Feinstein LLP, cautions that "collectors today need to be very sensitive to the possibility that an artwork or antiquity may be stolen or that an incomplete or suspicious ownership history may raise questions about the title to the work and will most certainly affect the work's value or marketability."

If a buyer does buy an artwork that is later proven to be stolen, the painting is returned to the original owner, and the buyer may not be compensated for their losses. Noh therefore recommends that all her clients pay an small fee to the art loss register, who can run a check in their database to see whether they have any records for the artwork they're interested in purchasing. While Noh admits that the database "isn't perfect—and it doesn't include every stolen artwork in the entire world," it does combine the law enforcement records of Interpol, Scotland Yard, and other private parties who have listed their stolen works, making it "a relatively comprehensive database." In addition, Noh states that all auction houses use it to verify that the pieces they're selling haven't been stolen and that it's a good idea for art collectors to do so if they're purchasing privately on the secondary market.

Another primary reason that art collectors choose to hire an art law attorney is to set up a non-profit foundation or trust to keep their art, which can serve long-term legacy and estate-planning goals. First and foremost, the foundation "should be driven by a particular charitable purpose," says Megan Noh, illuminating that "there is a myth perception that this is a simple way that somebody with a private collection can avoid paying sales tax."

Despite this, housing your art in a foundation does offer a myriad of tax benefits, as a type of 501 C3—a federally tax-exempt entity. For example, Pamela Grutman illuminates that "for gifting and tax purposes you get a full, fair market value deduction for property contributed to a qualified organization, which can be the collector's very own private foundation." This is particularly useful if you have been gifted an artwork in the past that has significantly appreciated, as you can "dispose" of the artwork in the foundation without incurring capital gains tax, or if you want to avoid the artwork's inclusion in your estate.

Moreover, suppose your foundation decides to sell a work. In that case, they can avoid capital gains tax—or, if the foundation wishes to purchase a piece, a collector "could make a cash contribution to a nonprofit, get a full deduction or income tax deduction for their contribution, and then the organization could go out and buy the work" says Grutman.

However, Grutman cautions that "private foundations are subject to very complex rules in the Internal Revenue Code," which the foundation must adhere to in order to avoid unexpected tax consequences. Megan Noh expands, saying that "there will be adverse tax implications if you start using money—or generating money—from things that are not associated with the charitable mission." In this instance, consulting an art law attorney is essential to allow you to mitigate long-term tax issues and remain tax compliant.

Moreover, to set up a foundation, you must first be recognized by a Bureau of Charities—usually for the state where the company is incorporated—before submitting the paperwork to obtain 501 C3 recognition. All in all, this process can take a couple of months, and can be pretty complicated. However, from the setup to structuring and working on specific projects in line with the foundation's aims, art law attorneys can help their clients to navigate the trials of creating and maintaining a foundation.

Another type of wealth transfer vehicle that art law attorneys deal with are trusts, of which there are about a dozen different types, according to Pamela Grutman. She stipulates the necessity of having a legal professional advise you on the correct type of trust and determine if it is a suitable vehicle for your collection.

In terms of estate planning, a trust controls how property is transferred, potentially for multiple generations. As a result, you can instill conditions in a trust that "really won't be in a will," Grutman elaborates, as you can lock in the direction of transfer of the collection so that it will be kept in the family for generations to come.

There are several different types of trusts, including an LLC, or a partnership, and the founder "may want to wrap those up in something called a family limited partnership—or a family limited liability company—which prohibits transfers outside of the family, without everyone's agreement."

With regards to the latter, Grutman reveals that she has set up family limited liability companies into which an art collection can be put, allowing a large family to enjoy the tax benefits associated with fractional ownership, "fractionalizing the interest in $15,000 amounts, and you supposedly gift it over the year" as Grutman explains, made possible by the annual gift tax exclusion amount, whereby donors can give a donee a $15,000 per year tax break.

At every step of the art collecting journey, from buying art and building your collection to engaging in legacy and estate planning, an art law attorney can be an asset, helping you to mitigate tax at every stage and keep the cost of maintaining your passion low while ensuring that the future of your collection is secure.

Chapter 11

Mentors to Art Collectors

A portrait of a man who loves to help his friends discover exciting, new African American talent.

DEMETRIO KERRISON—THE MENTOR CONNECTOR

Demetrio "Dee" Kerrison, who lives in Southern California, is a highly respected art collector and advisor, financial executive, and board member for numerous artistic nonprofits. With a particular passion for art from the African diaspora, Dee has been making waves in the art world, highlighting and disrupting the imbalance of Black art within the space.

Growing up in New York City, Kerrison recalls that art was always a massive part of his life. In elementary school, art was a part of the curriculum. He remembers taking school field trips to tour the Metropolitan Museum of Art and other places of artistic renown. Living in

New York meant that he had access to some of the most important museums on the planet, which he visited on his own whenever he had the chance.

In his adult life—at the beginning of his art collecting journey—Dee Kerrison made a life-changing move to Southern California with his wife, Gianna. Kerrison admits that, at this time, he had to find a way to fill his days with joy, so he began to collect photographs when photography was just starting to become significant in the art market. Unbeknownst to him at the time, this marked his first foray into the art world in a professional capacity.

From here, Kerrison and his wife began to build an art collection with the help of a consultant, and soon afterward they joined a nonprofit collective in San Francisco, where he "fell in love" with the city and its rich culture. This nonprofit was San Francisco Camerawork, an organization that supports artists using photography as their medium. Each year, the collective held a fundraising event where professional photographers would be brought in to donate their services to the cause together with documentary and fashion photographers.

This made it possible for people to pay only a nominal fee to have world-class photographers take their photos. Kerrison remembers how this became an ongoing Mother's Day event in his household where he, his wife, and their child would go and have their photos taken, a tradition that lasted for around twelve years. This was an opportunity to meet hordes of artists, and this helped Kerrison to establish himself within the artistic community.

As a former "urban kid," as Kerrison describes himself in an interview, he found the transition to Southern California difficult, so he would often visit New York to satisfy his craving for the arts. On one of these trips, he went to a show put together by Thelma Golden, director and chief curator of The Studio Museum in Harlem. This show, called *Frequency*, displayed the works of "emerging, cutting-edge Black artists" and was "mind-blowing" to Kerrison as he came face to face with the works of Wangechi Mutu and many of the most renowned Black artists of today.

Kerrison then met up with a dealer in California and confessed, "I want to buy some of that art; that's some of the most amazing stuff I've ever seen." To this, the dealer, according to Kerrison, laughed him out of the gallery, informing him that there were long lists to buy their work. This opened Dee's eyes to the culture of the art world and its vast potential.

Later, Kerrison was to join the board of a nonprofit, the William H. Johnson Foundation, that awarded a $25,000 jury prize to an emerging African American artist. One of the artists who did not win was Mark Bradford, one of the most successful Black artists today, which hints at the caliber of artists who competed for the prize. Through his position on the board, therefore, Kerrison was able to meet with and befriend an incredible array of artists who are at the top of their careers now "before they blew up," and really—as he puts it—"before Black art was a thing." Due to his position on the board of several nonprofits, he met a host of other influential people in the art world, such as Eungie Joo, who is now one of the chief curators at SFMOMA.

Kerrison boasts that he knows these people "socially," and they advised him on what art to purchase. Newer members of the artistic community call him and say, "I want your thoughts." More than seeking advice on purchasing art, players in the art world also ask him financial questions, which he enjoys helping out with. Kerrison admits he loves to help people—an ideal quality to have as an art advisor.

Kerrison also serves on the board of advisors at the Hammer Museum that "makes decisions around the museum's programming, and what gets into their collection." Kerrison uses his influence to ensure "that artists of color are represented in museum collections."

During the interview, Kerrison recommended a book by Dr. Bridget Cooks—*Exhibiting Blackness: African Americans and the American Art Museum*—which documents the African American experience with museums from past to present. Kerrison says that he recommends the book to everyone who asks him, "Why do you collect art of the African diaspora?" While Kerrison admits that, although a lot has changed for African American artists over the past few decades, fundamentally, Black artists represent a paltry 2 percent of museum collections nationwide. He does allocate credit to The Hammer, though, for increasing this percentage to 8 percent, and they're looking to increase that even further.

Another nonprofit where Kerrison served on the board is The Mistake Room, a noncollecting art space, and yet another is the Noah Purifoy Foundation. Noah Purifoy, as Kerrison clarifies, was one of the early assemblage of artists in the 1960s that "routinely featured race and Blackness in his work." One of the great things about the foundation, according to Kerrison, is the people on the board—including one of the founders, Sue Welsh, and board members Ed Rushca and Joe Lewis, a professor at UCI. More artists have since agreed to join the board, including the notable Elliot Hundley and curator Jill Moniz.

As for Kerrison's collection, he has acquired artworks from Charles Gaines, Glenn Ligon, Gary Simmons, and the latest rising star in the African Diaspora art scene, Amoako Boafo. Kerrison credits this latest acquisition to his friend, who told him to drive down to Los Angeles to a gallery to buy this emerging artist's work. Trusting the word of his friend, Kerrison drove to the gallery and ended up paying $4,000 for one of Boafo's artworks. That year, as Kerrison recalls, Boafo "rose like you would not believe," with one of his recent artworks at auction selling for one million dollars.

While Kerrison and friends mutually share their knowledge, one of his closest friends in the art world is Elliot Barnes, an American art collector living in Paris who regards Dee as his mentor. When he discovers a new artist that he's excited about, Kerrison will make his purchases and call Barnes, along with one or two others, and tell them to buy those works, admitting that he takes "great pride in sharing his wealth." He notes that by sharing his discoveries, he's "supporting the artists" as well as "helping his friends"—and it all comes back to him.

In addition to owning a selection of impressive artworks, Kerrison hosts shows to exhibit artwork he finds stimulating. His most recent show—which he co-curated—was at Fullerton College in Orange County. His friend, a teacher at the college who sought to "bring LA to Orange County" for the kids who had never been to Los Angeles to see a major art exhibition, helped conceptualize the exhibit.

Kerrison focuses on art from the African diaspora, though he is not restricted in his choices. He also owns artworks from Andy Warhol and Elad Lassry, to name a few non-Black artists, because he loves to see himself represented. He admits, "I want to see myself on the walls." Elaborating further, Kerrison expands this by saying he enjoys work "where Blackness is exalted; where Blackness is front and center" and loves work that speaks to the "political times."

Leading on from this, Kerrison says that he once got into a discussion with a Latin American museum director who felt that Black artists should pull back on talking about everyday issues concerning racism despite the fact that, as Kerrison notes, "that's what artists do." Artists comment on their daily experience of life, and the art they create is about "what they're feeling." The museum director referenced, "Black male representations of masculinity in contemporary art," a Thelma Golden show from the 1990s to back up his point, stating that the African American artists exhibited there weren't successful because their subject matter revolved around Blackness and racism. Ironically, that very same museum director has gone on to team up "with other galleries to do shows representing Black artists."

As Dee Kerrison continues to move forward in his pursuit of incredible artworks produced by the African diaspora, he will continue to spread his influence on the boards of various nonprofits to ensure that Black artists are seen, heard, and not taken advantage of. And, as part of the process, he will continue to help his friends discover exciting new African American talent.

Donna Thompson Ray—Why Art Appraisals?

When you are a passionate art collector, you may tend to think about your artwork's aesthetic and sentimental value, focusing on their uniqueness, on the histories of the artists who made them, and on their technical quality. The economic value of art is also crucial, but one does not always have the expertise or the time to study it in detail and keep up to date with the market trends or even just changes in legislation and taxes. That is why the critical figure of the art appraiser exists. They are professionals who have turned their passion for art and their knowledge of the art market into a practical, functional, and no less exciting job.

There are many reasons why people turn to engaging with an art appraiser. They will be important during times of the "four Ds": death, debt, divorce, and disasters. These are the four keywords that govern the mental calculations, the Rolodex, of personal property management. People may need to evaluate an estate for tax purposes after a death or for a divorce. They could use them to secure a loan or want to know the amount for insurance coverage in case of a disaster. Life is made of unforeseen events, and a personal property appraiser becomes crucial to handle these delicate moments with peace of mind.

However, when you own an art collection, the need for an appraisal takes on other connotations. An appraiser specializing in the fine arts sector then becomes an optimal choice well before an emergency, even during the collecting phase. In particular, the figure of an art appraiser specializing in insurance appraisals could be helpful in making proper cataloging of your artworks and determining their precise value. It could be necessary in case of damage or simply to know their market value and make forecasts.

For example, some factors that may affect the appraisal of an art object could be whether the artist who made it is a listed artist (i.e., an institutionalized artist, who has exhibited in museums or international exhibitions, who is represented by an art gallery, or whose catalogs have been published). In other cases, it may be necessary to assess the genre of the work within the art market, considering that it is extraordinarily fluid and changeable: artworks that were deemed to be vibrant and valuable in the past may well no longer be so today. For this reason, a good tip would be to redo the appraisal every three or four years on average to be constantly updated on changes of your artworks' market value.

"Good insurance brokers and underwriters are important to help protect and grow your collection."

The documentation provided by an art appraiser is a detailed report that identifies the history of ownership, determines condition, and establishes the value of the entire collection, based on market data, "piece by piece." The task of the appraisers is similar to the work done by the registrars and curators in museums and public collections. The report must include a detailed description of all the properties, accompanied by photographs. Besides, it must necessarily include the limiting conditions under which the appraisal has been done (for example, whether the work of art in question is framed behind glass), the bibliography of the sources you referenced, and the purpose of the appraisal.

Appraisal reports are for "intended user(s)." To be considered valid, it must always be provided in full. Therefore, here's some relevant advice for collectors: when you purchase an artwork, make sure that the appraisal report that is shown to you is complete and not just an excerpt; otherwise, it will not be considered valid documentation!

The US Congress strictly regulates the art appraiser profession. A qualified professional must adhere to USPAP (Uniform Standards of Professional Appraisal Practice). The Board of Appraisal Foundation carries out the "congressionally-authorized standards" of the valuation profession, including the administration of USPAP. This background, of course, can be supplemented by a plethora of other valuable credentials or qualifications. An art appraiser can be an art historian, an artist, a curator, and much more!

In addition, select a highly qualified art appraiser, who is a members of one of the three most significant appraisal associations: the American Society of Appraisers (ASA), an interdisciplinary association that includes business valuation appraisers, appraisers who work with real estate, jewelry, as well as personal property and fine arts; the Appraisers Association of America (AAA), based in New York City, which includes fine art appraisers, dealers, and art researchers; and the International Society of Appraisers (ISA), whose membership includes those specializing in antiques. You can be sure that he or she has completed many hours of appraisal work and numerous examinations and required continuing education courses. It might also be helpful to rely on knowledge and references; much of the work of art appraisers is done by referrals. And last but not necessarily least, choose with passion! An art appraiser can be highly skilled, but they must add an authentic love for objects and material art to expertise.

The art appraisal is an exhaustive inspection of the art collection, better if conducted in person. It starts with a documenting phase, where the appraiser strictly documents the artwork's existence, measuring it, photographing, and reporting its structural conditions. It is essential to attach any evidence that may be relevant, from the frame conditions to the front and back photographs. This can be vital in case you require an appraisal to sell your artwork at an auction.

Also, during the appraisal process, the appraiser searches for information regarding the work's provenance: how it was purchased, information regarding the previous ownership (especially if famous), whether it was in catalogs or exhibitions. A comparison with similar artworks in the current market could also be helpful. Everything becomes relevant to increase the value of an art object!

The art appraisal is a service of cataloging and inventory, and it is imperative to establish the art collector's purpose with the appraiser. Whether the assessment serves to verify insurance coverage, for a potential sale of the collection, or estate planning, all information is of interest to the appraiser before conducting the complete task.

The cost and timing of an art appraisal are variables depending on the state of the collection in terms of documentation, conditions, the notoriety of the artists, and scope. It can generally take six to eight weeks, depending on the project. Many appraisers work on a flat rate regarding the costs, others on an hourly rate. For example, the average rate of an art appraiser in the greater New York City area may be $250–$350 per hour. It is not an inexpensive job, but it is calibrated to the experience, skills, and time required by the task. Collecting art while managing it wisely is a process that pays off in the long run.

An art appraiser knows the art market in depth as well as the historical and artistic value of the artworks and the intrinsic passion of collectors. For this reason, there are three tips to keep in mind if you want to make both the appraisal easier and grow your collection knowledgeably:

1. The importance of conditions. It is vital to preserve works of art in optimal conditions. The temperature of the rooms should not be too hot, cold, or humid; the pieces should not be exposed to direct light or placed near heat sources. Collectors must be

parallel curators, conservators, and registrars of their collection, and their house is their museum!

2. The work of cataloging starts from the collector. It is crucial to keep up with the date, the documentation of your collection, receipts, items, and provenance. Cataloging on your own is functional but also a very satisfying task.

3. Be patient. No interesting discovery can happen quickly. Similarly, the work of appraisal can be time consuming. It integrates practical skills and a good deal of research, and like all research, you do not know where it will lead! Having patience is a critical concept to build and manage the best art collection.

Consumer Friendly Resources

American Society of Appraisers, https://www.appraisers.org

Appraisers Association of America, https://www.appraisersassociation.org

International Society of Appraisers, https://www.isa-appraisers.org

The Appraisal Foundation, https://www.appraisalfoundation.org

Chapter 12

Why Board Seats Matter

When we see how board seats represent power, money, and connections to the people who monopolize them and perpetuate the status quo, we can understand what African Americans have to gain by holding museum board seats. Every African American who does hold a museum board seat can loosen the tight grip on power that institutional White supremacy has claimed since these museums opened their doors.

A Quest to Champion Diversity at Every Level

In art museums around the country, boards and committees have looked relatively uniform back to the time of their founding. This does not make them so different from most other positions and offices of power in the United States, but at museums, it takes on a unique type of destructiveness because museums should stand for culture, heritage, creativity, and spiritual fulfillment.

Museums make a difference in people's lives, leading to long-term negative consequences when they maintain and support destructive powers and class structures. Representation in art galleries is similar to that in museums: "Black and brown artists have only begun being represented by blue-chip galleries in the past five to ten years," I stated in *The Black Market*. Therefore, it is imperative—and productive—to examine how all of this works, looking past the prestige of museum board seats and asking ourselves how it all fits together. What do board seats mean to those who hold them, and why should we all take notice of that?

For all those who see that we need to do more, these board seats may seem at times like a secondary concern. A board seat is, after all, only a single position directly impacting only a single person. For the sort of broad, large-scale change that we know we need to initiate, it may sound myopic to think about what we can do to install one person into one position of power. However, this is the wrong way to look at board seats. As much as trickle-down economics has proven itself to be farcical over the last few decades, power is cumulative. Power begets power, meaning that by fostering and demanding power in the form of museum board seats, we can expect the results to reverberate over time.

To understand why all of this is so, we need only to look at what board seats have come to mean who those who do hold them and how they represent power, money, and connections to people who monopolize them and pass them down and around to the people who look and talk like them. We can then also understand what African Americans have to gain by holding museum board seats.

First, museum board seats represent money. Those who hold them have to meet certain wealth thresholds first. Looking at museum board seats, you see not only White people but exceptionally wealthy White people in particular. In fact, museum board seats have become metrics by which the wealthiest White people gauge each other. This puts a value on them over and above their influence and power. To hold one is to find exposure to more opportunities to accumulate generational wealth, immersed in a world where that is the norm.

In addition, museum board seats have become important tools for practicing nepotism. When someone holds one of these seats, they decide the tone and tenor of the museum. They offer patronage, and in the same way that the Pope commissioned Catholic imagery for the Sistine Chapel, you can be sure that they will support and encourage art that looks and sounds like their own experiences. This serves to cut out everyone else, leaving any experiences unlike their own to fade away into oblivion. A museum board seat, as a tool for practicing nepotism, is therefore also a tool for exclusion.

It is also true that museum board seats are tools for practicing cronyism. While many museum board members will use their power and influence to favor those who look and sound like them for no reason other than comfort and their supremacy-based worldview, they will additionally use their board seats to perform favors for people of power who can offer them something in return. They become trading chips, nothing more than one more asset to pitch to the highest bidders. This, as you know, will never include those who hold little or no power.

At the center of all this is the never-spoken reality of the oldest and most prestigious museums: White supremacy. Institutionalized at colleges, in government, in banks, and on Wall Street, White supremacy has also found a warm welcome in museum board seats. Its perniciousness slides down from one holder to the next, each tacitly promising to uphold and celebrate the same culture of hate, exclusion, and oppression of their predecessors. The old ways become the unquestioned ways. When museum board seats remain the purview of wealthy, powerful White elites, they remain vehicles at the disposal of rich, influential White people's interests.

These seats are critical. Whoever holds them decides what they will represent. When museums fail to prioritize diversity from the boardroom down, it becomes all but impossible to stand by promises for diversity throughout the museum. From artists to technical employees, those who work at the museum are likely to look like those pulling the levers at the highest levels.

In consequence of all this, an African American who holds a museum board seat is in a prime position to offer aspirational leadership that champions diversity at every level. As Alison Gilchrest, director of applied research and outreach at Yale University's Institute for the Preservation of Cultural Heritage, puts it, board seats are of equal importance to training and collection in equity and social justice efforts.

Wealthy, powerful, well-connected people rely on

board seats to push back on these causes as well. They carry on the anti-equity, anti–social justice tenets of institutionalized racism by those who have bestowed power upon them. While it would make sense that board members would feel responsible to serve the communities that their museums call home, we need to remind ourselves that their communities may not be geographic and that, in fact, the communities with which they identify are likelier the wealthy, powerful, tight-knit groups of established families from which they hail.

The effects are undeniable. Board seats bespeak prestige and status and define social class—but this is not merely a thing of ego. Think of everything that goes along with social class, from the cars that people drive to the education that people can access. Every African American who holds a museum board seat can alleviate the symptoms of injustice by making decisions from the point of view of justice and equity. Even the mere act of replacing an elite member on a board is radical because it is one less voice lending its strength to institutionalized racism.

In 2020, *The Chronicle of Philanthropy* announced a $4 million grant to the American Alliance of Museums (AAM). The express intent was to foster diversity on museum boards. In their announcement, they made a point that speaks to this issue clearly: 46 percent of American museums have boards that are almost 100 percent White. While museum boards are surely not the only bastion of institutional racism in America, this statistic should leave no doubt about the massive amount of room for change and improvement.

Of course, this leads to questions as to how African Americans can start working toward claiming board seats. The first step in that direction is to find ways to play an active role in the museum. There are regular events, festivals, exhibits, and showings that African Americans can attend, offering their input and support and making themselves visible and known among the museum staff. This is a sensible path forward, but it is not going to be enough.

Responsibility for the exclusion that persists at museums nationwide rests in the current board members' hands. As long as they are using their seats as tools for nepotism and cronyism, and as long as they actively or passively prevent African Americans from holding board seats, they are moving in the opposite direction of ushering in change. By putting pressure on boards and bringing their composition to light, the community can bolster the chances of prospective African American board members holding the seats that they are ready to take.

In the long term, the fight for justice is going to transpire on multiple fronts. Everywhere that injustice has survived, there is an opportunity to wage war against it. As unassuming as they may seem to outsiders, museum boards will become one of those fronts. Who sits in which chair? Who calls the shots? Who decides what we celebrate and preserve? Who decides what art is?

These are the questions that museum board members are to answer, usually behind closed doors. Only when African Americans are sitting on the museum boards will the answers reflect African American interests and well-being. From the art on the walls to the names on the benches in the lobby, representation matters—in museums, just as in every other walk of life.

The way toward sustainable, lasting change runs straight through America's museums. Each seat is a route along the way; hold it, and you can speak into existence the America you want. Don't, and you can't. The question of board seats is as straightforward as that.

Raymond J. McGuire—Collector, Board Member, Mentor to Art Collectors

Getting his start as an art collector thirty years ago, Raymond J. McGuire joined an art board before he started to pick up pieces in earnest. That sparked an interest in him, inspiring him to look for artists who looked like him and find ways to support them. Although he knew little about the art world at the time, he devoted himself to learning. Slowly but surely, he developed his knowledge and began to visualize what he was looking for, deciding that when he was able to, he would collect from artists who looked like him, too.

It was a young curator who assisted Raymond's initiation into collecting. Sitting down for a drink with him, she walked him through everything she knew about Black American artists, pointing out which of the artists she had studied most extensively and which ones seemed most promising to her. Raymond explains how that meeting directed him to a book called *Six Black Masters of American Art* written by Romare Bearden and Harry Henderson that would prove to be a prominent influence.

In that book, he found his introduction to some of the artists whom he lovingly refers to as his "buddies": Joshua Johnson, Robert Duncanson, Henry Ossawa Tanner, Horace Pippin, Augusta Savage, and Jacob Lawrence.

Raymond's collection today resembles that list of artists. He owns several of Norman Lewis's works, along with pieces by Henry Ossawa Tanner, Charles Austin, Aaron Douglas, Alma Thomas, Sam Gillam, Sanford Biggers, David Hammons, Theaster Gates, Glen Ligon, Carrie Mae Weems, Lorna Simpson, Julie Mehretu, Debra Roberts, and Derek Adams, among others. Raymond has, however, stretched himself far beyond the confines of what anyone would call "typical collecting." As he puts it, "I got some wild stuff, man. So I'm going deep on this stuff." He points to some of his African art collection, such as a 300 BC Nok terracotta, bronzes from Benin, and a White Fang mask. His excitement about the art reflects a vigor about the act of creation itself and the role that each component plays in shaping culture.

Talking about how he decides which pieces he intends to buy and add to his collection, Raymond emphasizes the importance of studying and art education. He says that he learns everything he can about an artist's work before he makes a purchase, looking through all of the information and resources available to him so that he avoids buying on an emotional high. As he says, "You have to be a student before you can become a collector."

Raymond has made a wide-ranging impact on the art world as a board member, dating back to his first seat at The New Museum. At that time, Marsha Tucker ran The New Museum, and had established herself as a maverick curator, leaving the Whitney Museum of American Art to form her own venture. Because of his work on the board at The New Museum, other boards reached out to him, including The International Center of Photography (ICP) and the Whitney. In due course, he became the president of the ICP, serving in that position for just under a decade and serving on the Whitney's executive committee. Today, he holds seats on several boards: the American Museum of Natural History, Raintree, the Hunter School, the New York Public Library, the Studio Museum of Harlem, the Terra Foundation, and the Whitney.

As a long-time art collector, Raymond has taken to mentoring other collectors. He has built up such a vast network in the art world that the advice he has to offer is priceless to anyone who is just making a start of their own. To all of them, he offers the same advice first and foremost: "I tell them to do their homework, do their homework. You got to go do your homework; otherwise, you know, you've just got a sugar rush to somebody who says they're an artist." He reiterates how critical it is for people in the art world to approach their choices from an informed mindset, investing their time and energy into understanding what they are looking at so that they do not wind up making their choices on a purely emotional basis.

Looking out at the art world today, Raymond says that he would change the amount of cooperation that he sees among directors. He would like more exhibitions to emphasize representation, promoting diversity and inclusion by offering educational opportunities to young people who may otherwise not even know that the art world is there for them. In the same vein, he says that he would like to see curators learn more and become more aware of what is out there. One curator he points out as an example is Ruth Fine, who organized a retrospective of Norman Lewis at PAFA.

As a collector, Raymond has clearly taken his own advice, assiduously understanding what he has purchases so that he can talk about all of his pieces at length. There are many abstract pieces, figurative pieces, and representational art pieces within his collection. He glances back at his array and sees his development as a collector, remembering how Glenn was one of the first artists he collected and how Lorna James Little and Carrie Mae have both taken on particular significance for him at different times in his life. These artists are not only creators of business assets for him; they are his friends, passing along a surreptitious joke or a touching story, baring their souls to him, and asking him to do the same for them in turn.

In the long term, Raymond says that although he has not engineered precise plans for his collection, he does not intend to use the pieces to open his own museum. He states, though, that he has never sold any of his art—not even a single piece—which lends credence to the idea that these artists are his buddies. It is evident that, despite whatever valuation someone may put on his collection, all of the pieces within it have become such an integral part of him that it seems unlikely he will ever part with any of them.

Raymond's view on the art world is enlightening:

"You know, it is so inspiring to keep company with brilliance, with excellence. And as I look around here looking from room to room, I mean, we're blessed to be here. I say this with all humility because this is not how I grew up at all. People have afforded us the insight that we'll be respectful. This great art is genius. And you get so inspired during the rough times. And these people were not acknowledged, but the genius was still there. You see the influence, which people don't talk about. You can go back to the early 1900s and Picasso and the impact of African art on Picasso; look at *Les Demoiselles*, and look at the impact there. Look at how that's been reinterpreted. And you see just the richness of the culture, the royalty, and to be able to experience that daily and how it depicts the best of creative genius. It is inspiring. It's motivating."

Raymond says that he makes an effort not to take any of his collection for granted, cultivating gratitude for every piece day in and day out. He highlights Jacob Lawrence as one artist in his collection for whom he is supremely grateful. He explains even how his passion for art extends beyond the visual arts: he is a lover of the literary arts as well and talks about books as enthusiastically as he does paintings. He sees each of these media as part of our shared history.

None of this is fly-by-night for Raymond. He has dedicated himself to understanding the world through the lens of art. Let him speak, and he will wax poetic about the impact that art has made on his life. "That's powerful stuff that you see the entire history that you and I have now inherited, that we're the stewards of. You see that and just think about what our lives would be without that." He understands how hip-hop, far from being a separate thing from art, is part of this history and the legacy and beauty of our inheritance.

Referring to another of his buddies, Raymond quotes John Keats, whom he calls Johnny Keats: "Beauty is truth. Truth is beauty. That is all you know, on earth. And that is all you need to know." This seems as apt a quote as any for Raymond to embrace, so unabashed in its celebration of art as imbuing life with purpose and significance. He is not averse to quoting the masters of hip-hop, either. To him, these are all pieces of the same puzzle.

Reggie Browne—Collector, Board Member, Philanthropist

Growing up in Philadelphia and subsequently New York, Reggie Brown began his journey into art long before purchasing the initial pieces that would later come to comprise his impressive collection. Many an afternoon spent at the Philadelphia Museum of Art, his parents, and an uncle who encouraged him to start collecting lithographs all served to open his eyes to an extraordinary world of discovery and self-understanding.

When he was only twenty-one, Reggie started his collection in earnest. He was out on his own, his parents proclaiming that it was time for him to get an apartment, and, following their lead, he picked up lithographs of his own. Framing these pieces, he turned his apartment into a place that was all uniquely his, attending exhibitions and immersing himself in the learning process. Gradually, he picked up new insights and developed his own opinions over time, all of which added a unique flavor to his collection.

This would become a running theme in Reggie's life. Always a student, as his collection grew, as his stature grew, and as he took on official titles within the art community, he has markedly never lost his sense of wonder with art. Despite the incredible pedigree that one could associate with his collection and the enormity of his profile in the art community, he seems driven to collect art that he enjoys looking at—and that he would enjoy showcasing in his living room. As a student of art collecting, Reggie studied all of the catalogues that he could find, reading into scholarships and research wherever he could find it. He paid close attention whenever experts were speaking, understanding that there was something he could learn from each of them. This wide-reaching learning strategy that he recommends to other newcomers encourages aspiring collectors to keep their minds open to new works and to piece together all of the information gradually.

As a collector, Reggie has picked up pieces of all styles and genres, pursuing a perspective that is expressly his own, one that he says he defines based on curiosity. In one corner of his collection, front and center in his living room, there is an abstract piece by Moe Booker; not far from it, there is a figurative piece by Titus Kaphar, whom Reggie counts among his closest friends. He describes going through phases as a collector, at one point focusing on expressionist and abstract art and later on diving into figurative portraits.

Making sense of these phases, Reggie connects the art that he collects with his varying moods. He talks about reflecting on these phases by looking back on the works that remain in his collection, recalling how he felt at the time and why the piece made sense to him on an emotional level. In this way, he is collector centered in his thinking, saying that, "I think the collecting sensibility comes down to what resonates in response to the collector versus what the artist's intent was."

Speaking more specifically about his collection, Reggie notes that his oldest work dates to 1897, a Tanner painting that was part of a three-work series featured in a *Patha* exposition. He calls this work historic. Tracing his way forward, he mentions a Jacob Lawrence from 1947, a work presented in the *Whitney Biennial* and an Elizabeth Catlett from 1968, a cedar sculpture modeled after the young Black Olympian sisters who raised their fists to protest racial injustice. He also highlights a four-foot marble statue titled *Stargazer*, also by Catlett.

More recently, Reggie says, he has transitioned to collecting living artists, emphasizing those who are still working over those who have passed. As he puts it, "It comes down to just younger artists coming out of school." He has added artists such as Monica Ikegwu, a graduate of MICA, and others, noting that both are coming into prominence and expressing his desire to chat with them, understand them, and get a sense of who they are before he adds them to his collection. He follows this up by saying, "Then I'll turn around and I will talk to your curator and potentially load it to museums for distribution."

As to strategies for building a collection, Reggie says

that he would attend the National Black Fine Art Show every year while it was still running. He has also made a point of attending art fairs as they come up and building relationships within the community so that he can visit artists where they work and live. Still, he continues to go to dealers as a secondary option, contacting them as long as there is gallery representation.

Reggie talks about strategies almost as incidental to his manner within the art community. He says that he avoids art auctions, chiefly because of the high markup more than anything else. The relationships that he describes belie an uncommon place in the art community, one in which he can feel as if he is in the middle of things at all times, either contacting one of his close artist friends or their personal referrals for an introduction.

Of other collectors, Reggie says that although he has connected with many people in the art world, he tends not to think of art in the same way that many do. He has interacted with the JP Morgan corporate curator, describing the massive, eight-thousand-object collection and the curator's insistence on buying nothing that costs more than $50,000. In the same way, Reggie seems willing to take risks as he assembles his collection, in addition to buying pieces that speak to him.

When asked about mentors, Reggie shares that from everyone he meets, he learns something new. He embraces the same mindset he has maintained since beginning his art collection: listening to other people's thoughts and closing himself off to nothing. On top of that, he says that he listens to podcasts, taking in as much information as he can.

Within the art world, Reggie is not only a collector, either. He serves as the vice chairman of the Pennsylvania Academy of Fine Arts and as the chairman of the Board of Governors for their art school. A ten-year member of the board and an officer since 2019, he has progressed through the ranks very recently. He is also a trustee of Creative Capital, an organization that funds artists and offers support to artistic endeavors in the community.

Reggie brings the same insight and clarity that he brings to collecting to each of these board roles. He is also well aware of how crucial his position on these boards is. He says, "The boards are the ones that select leadership, and then leadership selects the curators. And without commitment to diversity, the institutions won't have a diverse approach to it from its collecting, or also its employees."

Because of his leadership positions within the community, Reggie can push back on the historic barriers that remain ingrained in the art world. He has also launched a scholarship, the Reginald Browne Christie's Education Funds, which Christie's underwrote as a means to fund students of color in the UK and the US. However, he notes ruefully, in the end this scholarship covered funding only for three students, one short of the four he intended. Nevertheless, the point was that it was possible.

Reggie speaks passionately about Afro-American inclusion in board leadership, and he sees it as a crucial step toward diversity, fairness, and representation in art collections. This, to him, is fundamental because of its moral and historical implications: Without curators to influence the collections in this way, significant pieces are missing from the narrative of American history. Put another way, collections without fair representation on their boards are likely to offer a distorted view of America.

Just as he offers advice to aspiring collectors, Reggie offers clear, actionable advice to those aspiring to join institutional boards. He suggests participating in committees associated with the institutions and purchasing a museum membership, which is typically affordable at less than a hundred dollars each. To him, young collectors should network with board leaders and committee leaders, making themselves and their aspirations known.

Referring more specifically to his networking and relationship building, Reggie points out that he is the largest African American donor to his institution, but then describes a serendipitous meeting with artist and friend Titus Kaphar, who was giving a TED talk at the time. He says that he saw an opportunity to reach out and help, hearing that there was a need for funding, and he decided to step up and do what he could. From there, the rest fell into place.

Talking about his place in his community, Reggie admits that within his development, his is the only Black family. He looks outward to the broader, encompassing community and says that there may be one hundred Black families in total. When he says this, it sounds like a reiteration of his point about the importance of leadership and board inclusion within the art community, moving immediately into a discussion of art in his family's life.

"My kids have grown up in art." He has raised his

sons and his daughter in the art world, encouraging them to learn how he learned, exposing them to art, and motivating them to pick up others' ideas and form their own opinions. He also mentions the George Floyd shooting, commenting that their understanding of art and heritage has helped shape their response to recent events within that context.

Due to the prominence of art in his family's life, these issues have been omnipresent throughout his children's lives. It is from this idea that Reggie expresses his wish for his collection: "When it's my time to go to heaven, and my kids inherit my collection, I hope they become custodians and understand the significance of it." He feels confident his children have already learned and grown from his collection. "But the legacy of what I've put forward is what is built in them to be the people they are: this is what art has done for them."

Dr. Joy Simmons—Contemporary Art Collector and Board Member

With four decades of art collecting behind her—and no plans to slow down as she looks to retirement—Dr. Joy Simmons, a retired radiologist and avid art enthusiast, is considered one of the most important collectors of African American art in the United States. After buying her first art print, a 1973 print by Elizabeth Catlett, while studying medicine, her thirst for collecting was whetted.

When Simmons was seventeen, she stayed with her uncle Ron Carter, acclaimed jazz bassist, and her aunt

Janet Carter, founding board member of Studio Museum in Harlem, a fervent art lover and collector who displayed many artworks in their home. This was one of Simmons's most meaningful experiences in her youth. It was her first time seeing African American art displayed in a home, a situation she remarked was "a very different experience from going to a gallery or to the museum." Whatever the differences, she revealed that African American artists—and artists from the African diaspora—were being celebrated in both homes and galleries, contrasting sharply with the past when few to no works representing the Black community were on display. Referencing Robert S. Duncanson, one of the Black artist forerunners who managed to overcome discrimination and make a career out of his landscape paintings in the nineteenth century, Simmons laments that the artist would not have had the opportunity to paint Black people in his day, famous as he was.

Her experiences with Janet Carter in New York, included not only viewing art but attending Janet's legendary soiree's where artists, writers, dancers and musicians would gather. She took her on studio visits with artists and where she realized the vast variety of work by Black artists, not only painting and collage but sculptures and films that one could collect. More than this, Simmons' aunt taught her that once you decide not only to purchase but to build a collection, that you find a 'focus' so that your collection can have a cohesive narrative. You decide if you want to focus on prints or sculptures or artists of a distinct time period, race or gender.

It should come as no surprise, then, that Simmons's

own home is full of art treasures from diverse sources, though they primarily originate from the African diaspora. Her preference is mostly in figurative work representing her people and her community, though she also has some abstracts in her collection. Simmons also comments on the effect that having children has had on her art collecting and the displaying of art in her home, saying that while her children were growing up, she wanted them to "see images that were reflective of them," as this wasn't a familiar sight for her growing up. As such, Simmons's house is enveloped in art and artistry. Genevieve Gaignard has done the bathroom, Lauren Halsey was responsible for the columns, and she even has a mural on one of her outside walls. There is "no space left untouched," she says in an interview with Artnet about her home.

Simmons's first advance into collecting was posters that she purchased as an undergraduate. She remembers that everyone was beginning to buy art—prints, as that was what they could afford at the time—with works by Romare Bearden and Jacob Lawrence topping the list. As Simmons got older, however, she "decided to change direction" from what attracted the crowd. Simmons started to interact with artists on an individual level and buy from them directly, purchasing unique pieces rather than accepting what was in vogue at the time. This was when she began to seriously forge the empire of artwork in her possession today.

Simmons doesn't necessarily believe that the artists she buys from have to come from a cultured background for her to connect to—and purchase—their work. When asked if it was important to her that artists are students of culture or literature, in particular, Simmons points out that excluding artists who don't have an academic background from her collection would deprive her of "a very different space of experience."

Today, and throughout her journey as a philanthropist and art collector, Simmons focuses on buying work that she believes is good—without considering the return on investment—and supporting the artists she believes in. Not knowing whether an artwork will be regarded as valuable in the future is part of the thrill of buying. Often, Simmons purchases artwork from young and emerging artists, saying that she finds it "fascinating and enjoyable" to watch them mature.

Some of these artists include David Hammons, whose work she bought in the early 1980s before it gained incredible worldwide recognition. Additionally, Simmons has a work painted by Sadie Barnett when she was just twenty, and in the ten years that have passed, Simmons has had such pleasure in watching Barnett's talents grow. Likewise, Simmons still has many young artists in her collection today, artists who have great ideas, think critically, do fine work—and who could be the big names in the art world of tomorrow.

More than this, Simmons has a particular affinity for contemporary art because she wants work that speaks to her time. Though Simmons has met artists such as Romare Bearden, who was prominent before her time, she notes that these artists were painting in an extremely disparate era. She prefers the work of artists that are "trying to grapple with our times," those who she feels are visually documenting our historical legacy.

In addition to her role as an unofficial mentor in the art world, Simmons is also on the board of several art institutions. Previously, Simmons was on the California African American Museum's foundation board, followed by a stint on the board of directors at ICA Los Angeles for a few years when it was still known as the Santa Monica Museum of Art. Simmons comments on the many incredible opportunities she was presented with to collect African American artists at this time, describing this particular museum as a "gem of an institution." She recalls how one of Mickalene Thomas's first West Coast shows was put on there and that Barkley Hendricks had put on a significant show there before his death. Additionally, the institution showcased international artists such as Elias Sime from Ethiopia. She attributes these awe-inspiring events to the fact that the institution, small as it was, was also progressive, listened to new ideas, and intentionally brought in contemporary artists.

Presently, Simmons is a commissioner for the Smithsonian American Art Museum and is heavily involved with art at Stanford University, her alma mater, working with the Cantor Art Museum's Anderson Collection at Stanford University. She says that it's both a place of historical art and a celebrator of contemporary works, having recently honored Jordan Casteel. Stanford had Carrie Mae Weems and El Anatsui speak at the university, while new Black artist Kahlil Joseph was the 2018–19 presidential resident artist at the university. In her position, she ensures that the students—especially students of color—feel free to interact with the museum and aims to foster an appreciative audience.

Despite the recent restrictions, Simmons still gets out to see as many art shows as possible. Recently, she was able to attend Ludovic Nkoth's show, which she describes as "beautiful," and saw Jeffrey Gibson's show at Robert's gallery as well as Cosmo Whyte's performance at Anat Egbi Gallery in Los Angeles. Despite the pandemic, smaller art-centered institutions and galleries have remained open, though by appointment only, and Simmons still makes sure she gets out to them. Simmons regrets that she couldn't attend the Pulitzer Art Museum to see Terry Adkin's show, but notes that there are many lectures and events via Zoom nowadays featuring works of art, though, admittedly, it's not akin to the real thing. Thinking back to a less complicated time, she reminisces about the art fairs in Venice, waxing eloquently about the diverse artists represented with artwork from all over the world, painted by people with vastly different perspectives, all of which were immensely valuable to her experience as a collector.

Simmons feels as though she's passing the baton down to the younger generation in art appreciation, buying, and collecting. She says this with some confidence because her daughter is a curator; that is, "someone else that's speaking and advocating for—and making sure—that art by African-Americans and from the African diaspora is shown at spaces, and celebrated, and researched, and written about." Simmons says of her daughter, Naima Keith (Vice President of Education and Public Programs for Los Angeles County Museum of Art and the co-artistic director of Prospect 5, a city wide contemporary art triennial in New Orleans), that although she doesn't seem to share her "collecting bug," she's putting on an art show called *Prospect 5* this year alongside doing a lot of work at the studio museum and even writing books to ensure that the research is there to support the art. We can expect that Simmons's legacy will be gracefully upheld by her daughter and those she has mentored during her time as a person of influence, a board member, and an African American art advocate over the last few decades. However, Dr. Joy Simmons will undoubtedly continue to bolster and influence the art world.

Chapter 13

Managing Your Assets

What should art collectors know about cataloguing and collection management, and what role do these tasks play in maintaining a valuable collection? Here's everything you should know.

CATALOGUING AND COLLECTION MANAGEMENT

Cataloguing and collection management are vital aspects of art collection. However, perhaps due to the unglamorous nature of the activities they entail, these tasks rarely receive the attention they deserve. Art collection, by default, focuses on the process, demands, and exhilaration of collection, often to the neglect of the work that must begin after acquisition and throughout the lifetime of maintaining the piece in the collection.

But, while this may often be the case, experienced collectors know that managing your art and keeping what you have amassed in proper shape will often be just as vital as collecting art in the first place. Apart from the fact that cataloguing and collection management should be a part of every collector's acquisition plan, there are also best practices to keep in mind to ensure that your art maintains and enjoys gains in its value.

Acquiring artwork is only the first step in an art-owning journey that may last several lifetimes, or a few years, at the very least. After buying art, your attention must next turn toward correctly cataloguing and then managing your collection. There is no precise definition of cataloguing or collection management. But, as will be clear from the get-go, it includes every action you take to set up a proper inventory of, protect, and manage your art collection.

From this definition, it would seem that there's no exact series of tasks or activities that are involved in collection management or cataloguing, especially since we're using broad words such as "inventory," "protect," and "manage." This is correct. Collection management is indeed a broad range of efforts that cover all actions you take to keep accurate records of your artwork, protect it from risks of storage and location, insure the artwork, maintain or increase its value, and be cognizant of the dynamics of eventual transfer. Cataloguing itself will be a minor part of what is involved in collection management. It applies most specifically to proper record keeping and inventory that lets you keep detailed accounts of the provenance of your artwork.

Since collection management and cataloguing involve such a broad scope of actions, many art owners find it more expedient to entrust the management of their fine art to experts. These experts are known as collection management specialists or art advisors. They will be in charge of overseeing and managing the art collection, with the added benefit that art owners can rely on their expertise for even better management.

Although it can feel like a lot of trouble, cataloguing and collection management play incredibly distinct and vital roles in the life cycle of your fine art. Whether this relates to the time the art spends in your collection or the overall life cycle, proper management can be beneficial in many ways.

At the outset, having a deep understanding of the types, provenance, and themes of the art you own can help guide the population of your collection. It helps if you keep a bird's eye view of the general direction of your collection so you can better decipher your tastes. Also, if your collection was initially intended to move in a particular direction, proper cataloguing and management is the most accurate indicator of whether you are on track or not.

Good collection management practices will protect your art against loss by allowing you to quickly identify the risks of storage, transportation, or disposition of your art. One of the tasks involved in cataloguing is learning the materials used in your art and any unique qualities they possess. Art can be incredibly fragile or may behave differently under different conditions. Comprehensive knowledge of your artwork will therefore help you anticipate possible risks and head them off. In addition, extensive art records let you quickly know if any piece is missing and where the piece likely dropped out of your collection.

Another obvious benefit of collection management and cataloguing is insurance. You are unlikely to secure competitive insurance for your pieces if you cannot assure the agency that you carry out good collection management practices. Keeping your artwork in good shape will protect your investment in the art and help facilitate future sales as well.

There's often a belief (sometimes a misguided one) that collection management and cataloguing is a practice that is best associated with museums and galleries. While it is true that these art institutions are more evident in their practice of art management, there's no basis for suggesting it is limited to only occurring in those contexts. In truth, everyone who collects art or has charge of it should practice good cataloguing and collection management. This includes traditional art collectors and families with art holdings. It doesn't matter if there are two thousand or two hundred pieces, or even twenty. Significant artwork should be protected in every way possible, and that includes implementing proper management practices.

Now that it's clear why collection management and cataloguing are important and who should practice them, let us turn to best practices in carrying out these tasks.

The first step in proper collection management is building an exhaustive catalogue of the artwork in the collection. This can be done in a spreadsheet, database, or a binder. The goal is to establish an accurate record that includes the following information:

❖ Name of artist (including their active dates) and the name of the piece

❖ Features of the piece, including materials, dimensions, and images of the installed work

❖ Date of purchase, with invoice and seller information

❖ Provenance of the artwork, including a record of previous owners and how it was transferred

❖ Condition report, including details of discoloration, striations, or chips in the frame

❖ Certificate of authenticity, when the work comes with one. This can affect the value of the piece, since there is proof it is not a replica.

❖ Inventory number

❖ Details about storage and location. Storage is where (and how) the piece is stored, while the location is where it is currently housed or displayed.

Most of the information you record in your catalogue will need frequent updating. This helps you maintain an accurate understanding of the state of your collection at any point in time. Some of the vital information that should be frequently updated includes the piece's value, location information, and condition.

Storage can be a tricky aspect of collection management. Apart from concerns over how best to display a piece, and whether proper arrangements exist, there may be a need to consider how best to protect the artwork. Unlike some art that you can plop on the mantelpiece or hang in a hallway, there are fragile pieces and will need considered disposition, both for storage and display purposes. This is where advice from a collection management specialist can prove vital. They have a wide array of experience dealing with different types of artwork and can advise you on how best to store your pieces.

A lot of the time in the art world, the value of a piece of art can be significantly affected by the artist's reputation. Understanding this correlation can be crucial to tracking fluctuations in the value of your artwork. This can also inform later purchases, help you refine your interests in the artist or similar artists, or place the works within an overarching cultural context.

Different types of software are available today that can help relieve some of the difficulty of cataloguing and collection management. Available applications are becoming more popular and often provide sophisticated tools to help you handle record keeping, track pieces, and even carry out virtual art showings. Most of the popular options also have cloud-storage capabilities, allowing you to access your collection from anywhere in the world and at any time.

Finally, it makes sense to consider either entrusting an expert with the entire collection management process or periodically consulting with professionals on the subject. For instance, consulting an appraiser every other year can help you accurately value your artwork. Working full-time with a collection management specialist will give you the benefit of their expert knowledge and experience, expertise that will prove vital in maintaining a viable collection.

The best thing about cataloguing and collection

management is you can start at any time. So, it may not matter so much that you are just starting on your cataloguing and collection management journey. The most important thing is to get off the ground properly, taking the proper actions to maintain a comprehensive inventory and implementing other best practices.

Chapter 14

The Phillips Auction

Phillips is arguably the most dynamic and forward-thinking auction house in the world. Conducted successively at its New York, London, Hong Kong, and Geneva salesrooms, it features the world's most important twentieth-century and contemporary works of art, design, jewels, watches, photographs, and editions.

AN EXCITING TURNOVER

In the recent Phillips auction on the evening of December 7, 2020, many exciting pieces from a diverse range of contemporary artists were sold, many of which went for a significantly higher sum than that estimated by art specialists.

Many works came from the collection of Pamela K. Royall and the late William A. Royall Jr., an assortment spanning a wide variety of artwork from some of the most well-known artists of the twentieth century to emerging and established Black contemporary artists shaking up the art world today. Almost forty artworks were sold—for hundreds of thousands to millions of dollars—and they were permeated with artworks from some of the most exciting Black contemporary artists, four of which emerged from the Royall collection.

One example is Mickalene Thomas's *I've Been Good to Me*, painted and signed by Thomas in 2013, which went for an astonishing $901,200, compared with an estimated value of $200,000–$300,000. Thomas is known for her visual examinations of the Black female identity, sexuality, and celebrity, and she habitually depicts Black women in collage-inspired paintings or mixed media artworks.

I've Been Good to Me portrays Thomas's muse, Qusuquzah, wearing a long, vibrantly patterned dress open along the center to display her long legs as one of the focal points. The changing color of the woman's left leg draws attention to itself amid the background's sea of textures and colors. The artwork has been created in Thomas's signature style, adorned layers of acrylic paint and engaging with different materials—in this case, the inclusion of rhinestones.

Another piece in this auction, also from the Royall collection, was a painting of Thomas titled *Portrait of Mickalene Thomas, the Coyote* that—compared with an estimated $100,000–$150,000—was sold for $378,000. Created by Kehinde Wiley in 2017, the portrait is one of eleven in his *Trickster* series depicting influential contemporary Black artists. In the portrait, Thomas stands with a coyote-esque dog on each side, her right arm raised to her chest with her hand placed over her heart—a proud, defiant pose, accompanied by a facial expression which proclaims: "Yes, I should be here!"

From the Renaissance to the nineteenth century, portraiture was at the height of its popularity. It was the chief method of documenting an individual or a family's existence, and the figures painted were overwhelmingly White. By the time the Black community began to achieve socioeconomic liberty by the twentieth century, enough for the opportunity to have their portraits painted, the medium for existential expression had shifted from painting to photography.

Therefore, in his *Trickster* series, Wiley claims an art medium from which the Black community was previously excluded and, by extension, claims that part of history for the community. Moreover, in choosing influential Black artists as his muses, Wiley adheres to the tradition of portraiture depicting influential historical figures. Some notable examples include Thomas Jefferson, President Theodore Roosevelt, and Sir Thomas More, in addition to countless monarchs.

Likewise, in documenting the influential figures in the Black artist community today, Wiley is establishing the community's place in portraiture. As the years go by, these paintings may become even more culturally significant as representing a transitional time for Black people. Alongside the past portraiture, these paintings must be preserved as part of the turbulent and ever-evolving history of the human race.

There is also a certain irony that this piece came from the Royall collection—the family name denoting royalty and the monarchy, signifying a privileged class. By showcasing these portraits, the Royalls have helped to facilitate the reconciliation of the contemporary Black community with the privileges that eluded them in the past.

Another culturally noteworthy piece that sold in the December 7 evening auction, coming from the collection of Payson and Helen Wolff, was Charles White's *Roots*. Created in 1963—the same year Martin Luther King Jr. gave his "I Have a Dream" speech—White's artwork shows a Black woman holding a massive bale of hay over her head. Her arms are strong, and her body is resilient even under the weight as she bears the load with dignity. White is known for a series of murals he painted across the nation, documenting the struggles—and the contributions—of African Americans to the United States. This artwork has withstood the test of time, having first been acquired by the Wolffs in 1965 and today reaffirming the continued significance of White's work in the art world. Originally valued at around $500,000–$700,000, the sale price ballooned to an impressive $877,000.

One of the more enigmatic artworks in this collection was painted by Titus Kaphar in 2008 and came from "an important West Coast collection". Estimated at between $70,000–$90,000, this painting went for the gargantuan sum of $365,400. In the painting, a lone figure can be observed sitting in a chair, wearing robes that suggest a religious personage, a hint strengthened by the book held in their left hand. However, a veil completely covers the face and obscures the shape of their body. The only uncovered part of the body is its uncanny hands, as its right hand is no wider than the figure's wrist, with unusually long, serpentine fingers, and the left hand grasping the book is obscured. This sinister figure is reminiscent of Bacon's *Pope* series.

One of the more abstract artworks sold in December, coming from an important European collection that housed it for the last few decades, was Jean-Michel Basquiat's *Portrait of A-One A.K.A. King*. Made from acrylic, oil stick, and marker, the portrait was created in a graffiti-esque style, depicting New York street artist A-One. The artwork challenges and reconciles "high" and "low" culture by portraying A-One. Basquiat describes the subject matter as "royalty, heroism and the streets." The painting sold for $11,500,000, within its predicted range.

From the property of "an important Asian collector," a text-focused artwork from Glenn Ligon, titled *stranger #67,* was created using oil stick, acrylic, and coal dust. Estimated at $1,400,000–$1,800,000, the artwork sold for $1,784,500. Ligon's textual masterpiece is a reproduction of the beginning of James Baldwin's 1953 essay *Stranger in the Village*, detailing his experience as a Black man in a Swiss village whose residents had never seen a Black person before. Ligon recalls that the essay, which inspired this work, "blurred the boundaries between the personal and the political." Likewise, Ligon blurred the text in his reproductive artwork, thereby reflectively blurring the boundary between the clear and the obscure.

Yet another piece from the Royall collection was *Selina/Star* painted in 1980 by Barkley L. Hendricks. A work in oil and acrylic on linen, it epitomizes Hendricks's practice of immortalizing cool, modern, Black and Latino figures in a contemporary style. The woman in this portrait in a soft blue T-shirt and sun-yellow trousers is a cool, relaxed figure against a block, mustard-yellow backdrop. With an estimated value of $800,000–$1,200,000, *Selina/Star* was sold for $937,500.

Amoako Boafo made his appearance with a new piece titled *Purple on Red* painted in 2019. Boafo's portraits, which are known for their vitality and texture, give the viewer a novel way of looking at and perceiving Blackness. In *Purple on Red*, Boafo depicts a Black woman in a purple outfit sitting on a red couch. The artwork is vibrant with the texture, depth, and variety of hues on the muse's skin, serving its most arresting features. Boafo says that his primary focus is in "documenting, celebrating, and showing new ways to approach Blackness." Estimated at $200,000–$300,000, the artwork went for $756,000.

From a private collection in New York came Vaughn Spann's *Big Black Rainbow*. Rendered in polymer paint and terrycloth on a canvas, the artwork presents a rainbow amid a blue, black, and violet expanse. This becomes significant when we consider a line from Spann, declaring, "I wanted to put Blackness back into the spectrum"—no doubt a double entendre, as Spann paints black literally into the light spectrum, subliminally promoting Black inclusion. While Spann's artwork was estimated to be worth $40,000–$60,000, it was sold for $239,400.

Jadé Fadojutimi's 2017 artwork *Lotus Land* also went for a significantly higher sum than was estimated, predicted to be around $40,000–$60,000 and selling for $378,000. Fadojutimi's artwork was an abstract piece layered with acrylic in vibrant shades of blue, emerald, turquoise, and yellow, depicting a fragmented landscape.

By far, the most exciting and groundbreaking sale at the auction, also from the Royall collection, was Amy Sherald's painting *The Bathers*. Here, two Black women in bathing suits stand confidently against a blue background, defiantly staring out at the viewer. Sherald—much like Kehinde Wiley—primarily produces portraits of Black figures, whether influential or unknown. Perhaps Sherald's most famous work is her portrait of Michelle Obama, America's First Lady at the time of production, that propelled her into artistic stardom. Riding on this reputation, *The Bathers* sold for an enormous $4,265,000, exceedingly above its estimated value of $150,000–$200,000.

DEFINING A TURBULENT HISTORY

Many of these artworks, produced by some of the most innovative and daring contemporary Black artists today, will define this period in history. As these provocative artworks gain greater recognition for their relevance and contribution to modern society, they will become integral to the culture to be preserved for future generations. Just as the *Mona Lisa* is thought of as a priceless masterpiece today, some of the artworks sold at this auction may go on to define this period of art history.

When an artwork is purchased, not only does the buyer acquire a piece of art, they acquire a fragment of the world's cultural history. Reflecting on *The Black Market*, I pondered, "through art conservation, we can preserve our cultural heritage for the next generation."

This small sample of the microcosm it was formed in should be protected so that future generations can enjoy and learn from the art in the same way that we have learned from previous ages. This is particularly significant when we consider that—compared to the time that has passed since the popularization of art, particularly during the Renaissance—Black artists did not have access to the wealth, resources, and status required to become internationally acclaimed.

As such, art history as it's written, which represents the African diaspora, extends only from the end of the nineteenth century with the works of Henry Ossawa Tanner to the present day, making each significant artwork even more influential in this niche of art history. "Children need to grow up with examples of Black excellence in this country and the diaspora at large," she said. "This is especially because of the negative stereotypes that we see in the media," I stated in *The Black Market*. This is particularly crucial to consider when many of these artists use their art to explore Blackness in the present context, in a changing social landscape, and at a time that is likely to represent a cornerstone in Black history.

ART AS WEALTH CREATION

As is clear from the results of this auction, artworks from postwar and contemporary Black artists are only becoming more valuable with time, with around 70 percent of the artworks going for higher than their estimated value. One of the most telling examples from this auction is Charles White's *Roots*, exceeding its top estimate by $177,000.

Despite the decades that have passed since its creation and the years since it was last sold, it has increased in value, testifying to its cultural gravitas.

Something that can't be overlooked after witnessing the results of an auction such as this is the enormous transfer of wealth from the buyers to the previous owners. From these pieces alone, tens of millions of dollars changed hands. Yet, this isn't the only direction in which wealth is transferred. Wealth is transferred from collectors to buyers in the form of the art, and the art is an asset in itself.

As an art services specialist at Bank of America Private Bank, Drew Watson observes that, while pre-boomer art collectors were focused on "connoisseurship and aesthetic appreciation," subsequent generations have "more of an awareness of the financial component of art," seeing it as a financial asset as well as an investment in philanthropy. As is clear from the results of the Phillips auction seen here, the value of an artwork can grow exponentially as the years pass and the artists gain greater fame, or a work's importance becomes more widely recognized, making art and auctions such as these an investment opportunity.

However, managing partner at Art Fiduciary Advisors Doug Woodham points out that, while luck and good taste can lead collectors to buy art that will increase in value, in the long term, "second-tier works by second-tier artists" are "unlikely to be great stores of value."

Another financial benefit to collecting art—which is only just beginning to be recognized—is the art lending industry, a sect of the art community that has grown exponentially over the last two decades. Art collectors are more and more often seeing the financial rewards of owning an art collection in addition to the personal and philanthropic benefits of purchasing such art.

Art can also benefit liquidity to its collector; if a collector takes a loan out against an artwork, they're more easily able to access funds than loans taken out for other assets, as the approval process is often much quicker. This is useful for real-estate investors, who often need to procure funds rapidly to secure a valuable real-estate deal, or even for professional art buyers and collectors should an exciting piece of art unexpectedly come on the market and require an immediate pool of funds.

Having said this, since artworks are a source of immense financial potential—and may account for a significant proportion of a person's assets—the financial responsibilities that come with owning a valuable art collection are also great. Compared to most other investments, artworks are more vulnerable to damage and theft, making it essential to insure your art. More than this, considering an artwork's volatile value in the market, a collector should regularly have the art valued and update their insurance policy accordingly.

"Donating to institutions shapes patrons' collecting practices. Ultimately, Black collectors who want more representation of work by Black artists can help remove obstacles by being strategic about donating work and making financial contributions to art institutions."

THE BLACK MARKET: A GUIDE TO ART COLLECTING

However, the paramount responsibility that comes

with owning an artwork or art collection is deciding—and acting on—what you want to do with your legacy. One option available to art collectors is to donate their artworks to charitable organizations or museums. If, while alive, the art collector cannot bear to part with their art full time, it is possible to arrange a fractional donation wherein the museum is given a percentage share in the artwork and is thus entitled to have that artwork for the corresponding amount of time per year. As a bonus, the collector receives an income tax deduction of up to 30 percent, depending on whether the artwork is donated wholly or a share is given.

Moreover, suppose a collector wants to donate an artwork or collection after their passing. In that case, the rest of the collector's estate receives a tax reduction based on the valuation of the collection at the time of death after being delivered to the nonprofit. When planning donations posthumously, the conditions of the donation should therefore be stipulated—that is, how the collector wants their art to be displayed and the rules pertaining to the exhibition—and this, ideally, should be agreed upon with the nonprofit or museum beforehand.

It is thought that most artworks and art collections will eventually be bequeathed, rather than donated, to family members, with artworks being deaccessioned from museums as part of "The Great Transfer of Wealth." This will entail an estimated $68 trillion to be bequeathed in assets and capital. Over the next decade, the wealth passed from baby boomers to Gen X and millennials will represent the most significant transfer of wealth in history, according to the 2019 Citi Art Market report. Furthermore, according to a study by Wealth X, illiquid assets such as real estate and art collections are expected to make up $1.9 trillion of this sum. To ensure the best possible future for an art collection, art collectors should always talk to their heirs so that they can ascertain the likely future of their artworks—whether it's expected to be kept as a collection or divided based on which pieces are desired by their beneficiaries, for example.

Unfortunately, we can expect that some younger generations may not share their predecessors' passion for art and may choose to sell the artworks after the passing of their donor. In this scenario, the new owner(s) would benefit from putting in place a strategic gifting plan, whereby arrangements are made to pay for the estate taxes associated with the newly acquired art. This would allow the new art owners to sell the art more conveniently than immediately after death since the latter suggests a "fire sale" and often generates a lower price for the artwork than its actual value.

However, since art is often an investment of passion—rather than an investment for financial gain—collectors who participate in the cultural preservation of our history, while supporting individual artists and the art industry as a whole, many find it difficult or unpleasant to consider their art in terms of finance, especially with regards to legacy planning. "I think we get stuck because of this idea of privilege and we think we have to have a certain kind of capital, but the capital may not be money. It can be a human capital. Artists love when you have their work because you know what it is, and you know who they are and you value who they are," stated Catherine McKinley in *The Black Market*.

That said, by being financially conscientious and consulting with their trusted advisors—including financial advisors, insurance brokers, accountants, and trust and estate attorneys, ideally people with a strong understanding of the art world—collectors can make the most of their acquisitions and accurately access art investment opportunities for their potential appreciation as well as any potential risk. By considering art as more than just a venture of passion and as a source of investment, an art collector acquires a financial benefit for themselves; they moreover ensure that, in the future, their collection continues to be as highly valued as it deserves.

Chapter 15

On aesthetics

MARIO MOORE ON COLOR THEORY AND WHY MUSEUMS MATTER

In the summer of 2021, Mario Moore emerged with a groundbreaking exhibition at Detroit's Charles Wright Museum. *Enshrined: Presence + Preservation* showcases dozens of the artist's early and current works. Blending drawing and painting is a testament to Moore's color mixing process. The artist's work features Black figures posed stern and tall, often connecting with the viewer's gaze, exuding a combined sense of intimacy and confidence that brings each piece to life. *Enshrined*, one might argue, is an attempt to highlight economies of social order within the context of Black America—a focus area Moore feels has been missing in the art space until more recent decades. Museums mean a great deal to the artist, whose work leading up to graduate school relied heavily on art history. The son of artist Sabrina Nelson, Moore grew up embedded in the Detroit art world before earning his MFA from Yale University in 2013. His early experience in the art world came from in-person interactions in his native Michigan, reading books, and visiting museums in his youth, museums which showcased European art history archives, western paintings, and the absence of the Black body. Moore has since made a career of addressing this absence with his unique color palette.

Painting, Moore learned from an early age, could broaden his—and by proxy, others'—perspective, presenting a world in which the bodies depicted in mythology or stories need not be exclusively white. Moore did start out drawing, though, and the *Enshrined* exhibition features mostly paintings but also a series of Moore's drawings from the mid-2010s. The artist is "probably going to be drawing forever", but he feels a greater pull to paint nowadays. His early experiences painting with oil occurred under the tutelage of Richard Lewis, a fellow Detroit artist and Yale alumnus, who mentored Moore between his sophomore and junior year of high school. "I started working in oils and found it to be hard," says Moore. However, he saw something there, and Moore tried again and again, honing his practice until he discovered acrylic paints as a college undergraduate. Acrylics, the artist explains, force you to work quickly, promoting a more stream-of-consciousness-style approach that dives deep into the subject of the work. The process of laying down colors—of creating the perfect blend—is next to impossible. And so, for Moore, in moving from acrylic back to oil, painting became more accessible than ever, and today, the artist has cultivated an innovative approach to oil painting.

Moore loves the way oil looks and the way it feels. It offers a multisensory experience, visual and textural, and museums, Moore explains, have allowed him to experience oil paintings in an entirely new way. With different media and a range of strokes, one can create a nuanced composition with a blend of oil and acrylic. Museum exhibitions allow the artist to witness how oil comes together, thereby informing his work. Where color is concerned, Moore notes that a person can distinguish specific artists based on their choice in the color palette, making color mixing a profoundly personal decision—a decision that, in Moore's case, pays homage to Josef Albers's color theory, a system ingrained in the Yale School of Art, based on the idea that color is contextual, present in a push-pull environment rather than in a vacuum.

According to Albers, color, in many cases, is not what it seems. Moore studied Albers extensively in graduate school, even completing a residency at the Josef and Anni Albers Foundation. What he learned most was the importance of simplicity in depicting the nuance of color. What this means is that in an Albers painting, the viewer might be fooled by the fact that one color is laid in the same value as the color next to it—yet the two might have different hues, one pushing the other so far back that a third hue seemingly comes forward. In Moore's work, the inspiration is clear. *Black and Blue* (2016) and *That Beautiful Color* (2016), both on view in Detroit, are significant in their choice of colors. The artist set out to explore the figurative language of the painting; in the former piece, a Black woman dressed in red fends off a police officer with a baseball bat. She is portrayed in color, while the man and the German shepherd in motion beside him exist exclusively in blue and white. Moore focused on time in this piece, his objective to convey a sense of the police officer returning from the past, but in a less gimmicky format than black or white or gray might exude, and with a subtlety that might also covertly reference the Blue Lives Matter movement. The painter created an ephemeral sense of space, an environment where it's difficult to place or contextualize his subjects because the background is essentially nonexistent. "They're floating in this mind space," says Moore, "because that's what it is. It's about this past and this present—the contrast between the red, the blue, and the warmer color of the background."

Meanwhile, Moore elevates his color theory expertise to unprecedented levels in *That Beautiful Color*. His objective was to create a dark composition while still conveying the shift between the Black female body at the center of the piece and the shadows of the background: the living room fireplace, the mantel, the two canvases adorning the walls. In the work, a woman sipping from a mug—dressed entirely in black—stands at the center of the canvas, the light on the woman's face and hands popping forward in the piece. The caveat in this piece, one might be surprised to learn, is that Moore didn't use a single drop of black paint—no matter that 90% of the work looks as though it would indicate otherwise. More than any other painting, this piece highlights the brilliance of Moore's color mixing and his reliance on the Josef Albers color theory to achieve a black effect in the image. The result is akin to an illusion, the realism of the piece existing in stark contrast to the colors the artist used behind the scenes, and the outcome is enticing. The viewer can't help but ask: *Can we trust what we see? Does the path we take matter, or is the result most important?*

"Sometimes if you use black paint—if you don't know what you're doing, and if you don't know how to shift the hues of black by adding other colors—then black becomes almost like a wall," says Moore. As a result, the viewer might not see into the space depicted in the composition. To create a more immersive experience, the artist steers clear of black paint altogether—to showcase the complexities of black skin, he has never once used it. Ultimately, Moore works to show as many colors as possible in Black people's skin tones, integrating as many hues as he can manage. The artist will use blues mixed with umbers, greens, and reds, creating different depths of the color black—a depth that the color black itself could never achieve.

Black, Moore explains, is a combination of all the colors. The artist considers this a beautiful thing, and the *Enshrined* exhibition would indicate the same.

KNOWLEDGE BENNETT: TRIANGLES, DIAMONDS, AND THE COLOR BLACK—REFLECTIONS OF THE SELF

In all art that catches the eye and makes a statement, some element stands out from all the rest. There is an idea or a message, a technique or an effect, something that transforms the piece into a memory—something that causes it to stick with the mind. However, in this untitled triangle painting, there are two standout elements: the color and the glimmer. Painted black, it captivates all who look at it, and then it seems to move, still but alive. Speaking to the artist Knowledge Bennett, you get a glimpse into what these elements mean but, even more fascinatingly, how they are as effective as they are.

Like most of Bennett›s painting, the triangle piece is without a name. As he continued to follow through on the concepts that inspired the series, he decided to avoid nomenclature altogether. His intention, by forgoing names, was to remove any preconceived notions in work. He wanted the viewer to experience the paintings, their colors, and their textures, only in terms of what was in front of them, without any of his outside input.

That was a critical decision: without a title, the paintings stand apart from the world around them. They are more like wide, open spaces, exact locations than points on a map. Bennett sees a connection between this choice and the more extensive history of fine art. He has drawn influence from his progenitors, who chose to cover canvases with black as well. Luminaries like Frank Stella and Mark Rothko consider his spiritual predecessors, laying the framework for him—though crucially, through the heart they brought to their work.

Bennett›s influences extend beyond America›s borders as well. He spent time in the south of France researching artists, particularly Picasso. He got from them, and the south of France that they shared, a sense of the vibrancy that had shifted the tone of their work. The experience was, as he puts it, "powerful." He glimpsed how their palettes had changed, how darkness seemed to define the northern part of the country, and he allowed that change to overtake him as well. One artist he met, a man more than 100 years old today, worked with black pigment for nearly two whole decades. To see that sort of dedication and that sort of practice was bound to affect Bennett.

The aesthetic spoke to him on a deep level. It was personal to him: he had always driven a black car, he had always worn black clothes, and growing up, he understood the color black as a cultural touchstone. It was apart from all of the other pigments. Even when he was honing his skills as a photographer, he would conduct heavy experimentation with black-and-white film. The minimalism called to him. In his own words, «It was something about the silence, from a black and white image, that resonated with me, having no color images. For me, color represents a sound. And blackness represents silence. So it would make me feel very at peace and at ease and in this tranquil state.» Adding to that, he says, "I›m not a colorist. I love the black and white, something very modern, or just black by itself."

When Bennett was just starting his work on the Black Paintings series, he put extensive thought into the shapes that he would use. At first, he selected traditional canvas shapes, mainly squares. There was a yearning inside him, though, to stretch himself outside the conventional, to see what else geometric shapes could offer him. The circle was intriguing.It was the triangle, however, that stuck.

Bennett explains that the triangle was alluring to him because of its place in sacred geometry. A symbol of spirituality, it enhanced the personal energy that he put into the series. When he was painting, it was a transfer of himself, from his mind to his hand to the canvas, and when the canvas was a triangle, it made sense. He expands upon this idea: "Take a look at the triangle. You have triangles within a triangle. And when you have triangles within a triangle, how I designed it, you have these inverted triangles, so you have the good plywood representing the positive, the inverted, meaning the upside-down triangle, representing the negative, but that›s also conveyed through the usage of the black diamonds, versus the non-usage, or the lack of the black diamonds, so all the triangles pointing upright are coated in the diamond dust, and then all the ones going down are lacking the diamond dust."

There, it turns out, is the third element that causes the paintings to stand out. It is their shape, it is their color, and it is their sparkle. He sees these sparkles, the diamond dust as glimmers underneath the light, as reflections of the higher self and the lower self. When the sparkles are visible, there is an ascendancy. Through invisibility, the dimming of the diamond dust, the spaces where it is absent, there is a return to the Earth—to, as Bennett says, "our animalistic instincts".

The series, ethereal as it may sound, has evolved from a place of tremendous emotion. In 2018, Bennett lost his significant other, his father, and his brother. Those losses, occurring as they did on top of each other, led him to take up diamond dust as a primary material in his work. He sees the absence and the presence of sparkles also as representations of friends and enemies. When the glimmer fades, there is a hazard, negativity to which he is calling attention.

Returning his thoughts to the color black and its prominence in the paintings, Bennett notes that there are two different types of black that he uses. He often prefers a bone ivory black, which he shortens to "bone black," but he has also used "mars black" frequently in his most recent work. He also points out a vast variety of black pigments available—each one sending its message, each one entailing its strengths.

He likes the browner tone that he sees when bone black is first applied to the canvas; the other black paints cone out bluish or greenish art first. His preference derives from the ethnic implication. He says, "Because we are Black people, we›re all different shades of brown. So, with that relationship between black and brown together, it goes hand in hand for me. That›s why I chose that one in particular."

Despite the evident importance of the bone black paint that he uses, if he were unable for some reason to access that specific paint, he would be able to move on from it. It is then that he delves into the wide world of black pigments, breaking down the science of pigmentation. Other artists, he refers to as "chemists when it comes to the color black." He exhibits a reverence for their devotion to their craft, though he says that he felt that approach would have been unnecessary in his work.

It makes his quick acceptance and willingness to move on from the pigment he has used for more than 200 pieces all the more striking. When he speaks about the pieces in the Black Paintings series, he speaks at length quickly. He goes in-depth about all of his choices, even speculating about the thought processes that have brought him to where he is in his work. Nothing is accidental. Every choice that he has made about the triangles, about the sparkles, about the color black, they have all come about after lengthy self-reflection—as well as research, both academic and in-person. He has traveled the world in search of the right and proper ways to create his paintings. In minimizing the number of elements in pieces, he has caused all three to stand out.

This is a feat when artists will spend their lives trying to create something in which even a single element will do the same.

That is the impact of Bennett's series. These paintings, emerging into the world without names of their own, grab onto the viewer and refuse to let go. One could get lost in the shapes and then, regaining composure, get lost once again in the diamond dust. Then, at the end of it all, the pigmentation is significant to the artist, a piece of Black culture analyzed and cherished. The brilliance of…

Chapter 16

The Black Brilliance

Black

> Color is a coating applied later on to the original truth . . .
>
> —Roland Barthes, *Camera Lucida*

> *(That) darkness is what I think about when I think of black. I would write the color black, but as every child knows, black isn't a color. Black is a lack, a void of light. When you think about it, it's surprising that we can see black at all: our eyes are engineered to receive light; in its absence, you'd think we simply wouldn't see any more than we taste when our mouths are empty. Black velvet, charcoal black, Ad Reinhart's black paintings, black-clad Goth kids with black fingernails: how do we see them?*
>
> —Paul La Farge

Whenever art history comes to a point when its standards

need to be reevaluated, and paradigms shifted, the black surface emerges as a symbol of negation, an absence of color and figuration, and the obsolescne of normative canons of representation and composition. Painting a canvas black seems to symbolize an ending of a phase and a return to the foundations of visual language.

The black surface indicated the beginning of nonobjective art when it appeared in Malevich's *Black Square* in 1915, and posed the question of institutionalized value in the dematerialized context of the 1980s art scene when Allan McCollum exhibited his *Plastic Surrogates*. The absence of color represented in these works differs significantly from the lack of light that color theory defines as black, and is frequently repeated by our high school art teachers. Anyone who has had a chance to stand in front of Mark Rothko's *Black and Grey* series and be taken into the sublime and inviting realm of those planes of black would never think of considering it a negation, let alone an absence or a noncolor.

By leaving aside the physics behind our optical system, we set the grounds for a phenomenological approach to the color black as the definite aesthetic presence, sought-after artistic means, and multilayered symbol it has been (and still is) throughout the history of our visual culture. This kind of approach takes us back to the very emergence of our aesthetic sensibilities and the stories of how our species began to express itself visually.

> absence is the figure of privation; simultaneously, I desire, and I need.
>
> —Roland Barthes, *Fragments of a Lover's Discourse*

For a long period of history, the furthest back we could search for written and/or visual accounts of our spectacle culture was antiquity. One of the favorite resources for many scholars searching for the beginnings of our (Western) culture's habits is Pliny the Elder and his *Naturalis Historia*. It so happens that this Roman philosopher located the beginning of visual art in a black trace drawn in charcoal: his story tells us of a young Corinthian woman whose lover was about to leave for a long journey. As she was saying goodbye to him, her gaze fell onto his shadow on a nearby surface, which immediately inspired her to take a piece of coal from the fire and make an outline of his features—thus creating the first-ever linear drawing. Whether or not this was an actual event in ancient Greece, we know that it in fact was not the first art piece ever created. The part of the story which is of interest to us, though, is the means and motivation behind the act: faced with the imminent absence of her lover, the woman reached for a visual substitute, a representation, a simple line in charcoal to stand in for the lost object of her desire.

A more factual, considerably older, yet no less compelling story of the first black line was not uncovered until the twentieth century. The cave paintings of Lascaux and Chauvet were discovered in 1940 and 1994, respectively, and made us much more aware of how deeply rooted our sense of spirituality, aesthetics, and desire are in the presences of darkness and light, earth and fire. Looking at those depictions drawn with earth pigments, charcoal, and even bone, we can almost understand how the ancient Greek mythology surrounding the idea of darkness, Nyx (from the ancient Greek: Νῠ́ξ, "Night"), as the mother of everything, came to be. The image we create in our mind's eye is of the Paleolithic artist living the dialectic of darkness and fire, using a torch to bring light to his lines, experiencing how the different shades of black, umber, and ochre emerge from the deepest absences of light within his cave. Finely stylized figures of horses, bison, and aurochs represented outlines of things sought and desired (similar to the Corinthian artists' lover), and are some of the most frequent representations found in the caves. The other kind of image was the proto-printmaking, or Paleolithic version of stencil art, located in Cueva de las Manos ("Cave of the Hands") in Argentina, discovered in 1964. These images were created by blowing dark pigments onto the wall surfaces, so instead of dark outlines on a light background, they formed hand-shaped absences in the fields of black and red.

In *Art and Visual Perception: A Psychology of the Creative Eye*, Rudolf Arnheim cites anthropological studies that dealt with what language can tell us about our relationship with color. The research shows that even the most elementary systems can distinguish between dark and light. In other words, they have names for black and white. When a third element is added, it is usually red. Visual arguments for this linguistic phenomenon can be found in the art practices of different cultures across the globe. Think of traditional West African pottery and fabric art, ancient Greek vases, early Christian and Buddhist frescoes, South American tapestries, and so on.

If we step away from fine arts in the strictest sense, the entire story of the written word can be seen as the story of dark shapes on light surfaces. In that context, contrast can be understood as the foundation of meaning.

Our use of black as a pigment, and more importantly, as a color, is rooted in our historical relationship with the surrounding elements, the elements we have been in touch with from the very start—earth, ash, coal, dust, and organic matter. The value of black was intertwined with its abundance and used in daily life; it wasn't until we started discovering minerals that specific (rare) nuances became symbols of power, wealth, and prestige.

As different shades of mineral-based pigments became part of our life, our palette became part of the system of market values and trading, and by extension added symbolic meanings. The easily accessible charcoal was no longer a source of exuberance compared to the rare and expensive ultramarine (lapis lazuli).

Apart from the distances needed to be traveled and the hard labor involved in acquiring some of the most prestigious pigments, another aspect of color as an artistic means became a determinant of value—the quality of craftsmanship. Various accounts of recipes, guidelines, and advice can be found in antique and medieval writings from Italy, China, India, Persia, and so on, covering topics like which kind of wood produces the most refined charcoal; which combination of resins, animal glues, and minerals give the best ink; and even which types of perfumes can be mixed in to add to the calligrapher/painter's experience.

The market value of black was raised considerably

when a much more nuanced, more elegant carbon-based counterpart of charcoal was discovered in sixteenth-century England. Graphite, the symbolic and literal heart of the pencil we take for granted today, created a small revolution in the history of visual arts. During the seventeenth and eighteenth centuries, England monopolized the production of lead pencils. The expensive material was in such high demand that miners and smugglers were willing to risk getting beaten for small quantities of it. In 1794, a conflict arose between England and France, which Victoria Finley dubbed "The Pencil War." Thanks to the efforts of France to create an adequate substitute for the English product, we now use the standardized HB system of signifying the hardness: the blackness of our pencils based on the amount of clay added to the mixture.

> One must respect black. Nothing prostitutes it.
> It does not please the eye or awaken another
> sense. It is the agent of the mind even more
> than the beautiful color of the palette or prism.
> —Odilon Redon

Late medieval and Renaissance art significantly changed both the practice of art and the role of the artists. The painter/sculptor was no longer a nameless servant of God but an educated professional, and in some cases, a heroic genius—the Renaissance man. Humanism underlined the value of rational, scientific thought, and a deeper, more objective understanding of color, and line was the new imperative.

On the one hand, the discovery of perspective brought out the importance of composition and planning, so the pencil and charcoal stick became extensions of the rational mind. New insights into optics and color theory laid a foundation for considering values and intensities, sources of light, and principles like chiaroscuro and sfumato, famously present in the works of masters such as Caravaggio, Da Vinci, and Rembrandt. One of the most significant breakthroughs of the period was oil painting—some of the oils we still use today we owe to the Renaissance.

Black Earth, Ivory Black, Carbon Black, Lamp Black, Mars Black, Perylene Black . . . It is unfortunate to try to explain or describe the subtle differences between the shades of black. Even good-quality photographs can be inadequate as the qualities of warmth, undertone, and transparency are dependent on the light, type of carrier, solvent, varnish, and so on. While some synthetic pigments have only recently been discovered (such as Perylene Black), we know from the writings of Giorgio Vasari that the Renaissance artist was familiar with many of the types of black we still use today.

Ivory black, one of the two carbon-based types, was famously used by Rembrandt van Rijn in most of his paintings. Carbon black is present in the darkest shades of Raphael's paintings. Carbon blacks were, and still are, the foundation for inks used in printmaking; relief printing, intaglio, and lithography presented a more affordable, democratic art form than oil painting, but their historical and artistic influence was by no means less significant. Artists known for their black-and-white etchings and lithographs were Albrecht Dürer, Rembrandt, and Francisco Goya.

Black is the queen of colors.

—Pierre-Auguste Renoir

Black is a force: I used black as ballast to simplify the construction.

—Henri Matisse

The discovery of black-and-white photography pushed painters into new modes of expression. Their experiments with color theory and optics, mixing and juxtapositions, led many of them to a temporary ban on black. The impressionists were intrigued by the ideas of light and primary colors. Except for Eduard Manet, most opted for blue and purple pigments to portray darkness and shadow. Henri Matisse, who wrote down many of his thoughts on color, quoted Pissarro, saying how the true strength of Manet's paintings was his ability to portray light by using black.

Post-impressionists and the subsequent movements—cubism, expressionism, and fauvism—were inspired by non-Western art brought back from colonies and distant territories, especially Japanese Ukiyo-e woodcuts and West African artifacts. These influenced the return of black pigments, solid contrasts, and thick, black outlines, which can be seen in Matisse, Picasso, Van Gogh, and many others. These formal borrowings did not necessarily consider the symbolic layers of meaning different cultures ascribed to their art. Still, they coincided with the turbulent historical context, and the color black served as a symbol of the darkness and suffering of war. In works like Picasso's *Guernica* or Käthe Kollwitz's *War* series, the archetypal relationship of black and white reflected the urgency of the artists' antiwar stands.

While different cultural and historical contexts have added further readings and connotations to the color black, its universal potency is undeniable. It was the symbol of darkness, death, despair, and the origin of all things, the birthplace of light (for the Paleolithic artist, for the Greeks, for Manet). In some cultures, it represents mourning and austerity and the death of the ego in some cases. At different points, it represented both the bourgeoisie and the working classes. It was both cheap and abundant as well as rare and prestigious. It was a symbol of the rational, objective mind and a symbol of rebellion and break from traditional modes of expression. It was at the same time a statement and a tabula rasa: an absence and a presence. The globalized society we live in today allows us to consider all of these facets of color without conforming to one particular code of interpretation. We can even still argue whether or not it is a color at all. The only constant we have to agree on is that this absolute absence of light is an unmistakable presence of meaning. And in that sense, it is brilliant.

Brilliance

The night is not the negative result of withdrawn

light but the joyous arrival of a dark cloak that replaces or covers the day. Night, according to children, consists of black clouds, which move close together so that none of the white can shine through. Some artists, such as Rembrandt or Goya, at least part of the time show the world as an inherently dark place, brightened here and there by light.

—Rudolph Arnheim

In his last work, *Remarks on Color*, Ludwig Wittgenstein wrote a series of micro-essays surrounding different qualities of color as a phenomenon. As he explained in one of the paragraphs, the idea was not to create an extensive theory of color but to look at the logic behind our notions of color. As our sense of logic is so thoroughly intertwined with language, Wittgenstein devoted a lot of the writing to how we talk about and/or describe colors. By language, we mean the universal logos, or the Saussurean langue (as opposed to specific languages or langue).

Which words do we use to describe the color? Which words would you use to refer to black? Most probably, we might go for deep or dark; in some situations, we might even say scary or use the phrase "pitch black." We would refer to some distinctive qualities of the color in an artistic context and use the words warm or cold, opaque, transparent, or matte to compare different black pigments. But would we ever call it bright? Wittgenstein probably would not. He wrote that black could not be luminous or reflective and referred to Goethe's theory of colors to prove that light can never come out of the darkness. Perhaps Eduard Manet and those of his contemporaries who admired him might disagree. Yet Wittgenstein insisted that the color black cannot shine and that portraying shine or glow was one of the hardest things to achieve in painting. He even wrote that mixing black into other shades made them less bright. But what do we mean by brightness?

In *Art and Visual Perception*, Rudolph Arnheim explains that the brightness we see depends, in a complex manner, on the distribution of light in the entire context, on the optical and physiological processes in the observer's eyes and nervous system, and on an object's physical capacity to absorb and reflect the light it receives. This biological capacity is called luminance or reflectance. It is a constant property of any surface. This makes perfect sense to anyone who had paid attention to what their high school art teacher was saying—the colors we see are reflections of light, and black absorbs all other colors. Ergo, it cannot be referred to as reflective or bright. But the term, much like another one we will be considering later on in the text, is dichotomous.

The quality or state of reflecting or emitting light is only one of the color's denotations. The historical understanding of black as a versatile means of logical thought and rationality comes back to us if we consider brightness in its other meaning: the quality of being intelligent or quick witted. As the presence of importance and foundation of all different shapes and interpretations, we can consider the color an agent of shedding light (upon).

I always felt caught between two kinds of black: that of the dirty and dirtying substance and that of the signs that miraculously emerged from it through the magic of wayward fountain pens, which, when dipped too deep in the inkwell, had a strong tendency to cover the paper with what used to be called "inkblots." Oh, the miracle of a clear and possibly elegant sentence emerging from the sticky ink and wending its way between the blots! It is the black of meaning wrung from the black of matter . . .

—Alain Badiou

Both linguistically and philosophically, there seems to be an innate connection between light and truth. Heraclitus believed our eyes were more reliable witnesses than our ears. Although a much more complex allegory, Plato's Cave seems to draw a parallel between darkness and access to knowledge and understanding. Why do we use phrases like "being kept in the dark" and "shedding light" upon something when we want to talk about knowing? If black is absorbent of all light, should that not imply it absorbs all comprehension? Do the paintings of Malevich, Ad Reinhart, and Allan McCollum represent an absence of absolute truth, having absorbed all previous knowledge?

Everything in the world results from creative and careful dosing of black as it is projected onto the formidable invariability of white. Anyone who hasn't experienced this, and sooner rather than later, will never learn anything.

—Alain Badiou

All of these questions come together in the story of how we might start considering the universal, versatile black as brilliant. While brightness connotes a quality of all surfaces, brilliance is something else, something exceptional.

Again, there is the dichotomy. "Brilliant" as referring to something incandescent, dazzling, and unwaveringly bright (the opposite of black?). And "brilliant" as well as genius, exceptionally bright and/or talented. The second interpretation brings us back to the idea of versatility and how it was understood in the Renaissance. Genius was the new kind of artist of the Renaissance, the polymath, the homo universalis. With the revival of ideas of antiquity, the Renaissance man was conceived as both the philosopher, the inventor, the master painter and sculptor, and the lonesome hero. Think of the mythologies created around artists such as Leonardo da Vinci and Michelangelo. These artist geniuses became the paradigm upon which the art world was based for centuries to come. A paradigm that is only now beginning to shift, as we are starting to consider all of the artistic phenomena overlooked and marginalized due to the heroes and canons. A later form of this kind of artist was the flaneur, the talented, curious, (often Parisian) poet and genius who spends his days exploring the poetics of urban space and searching for the aesthetics and symbolism within his surrounding society. The flaneur is personified in artists such as Charles Baudelaire, Edgar Allan Poe, Marcel Proust, members of the Situationists International, Oscar Wilde, and his famous quote: "I have nothing to declare except my genius."

Wilde used the term "genius" to refer to his brilliance, and such a meaning is rooted in the Latin language and culture and refers to the spirit of a person or place, a guardian deity, but also derived from the root -*gene*, denoting something which is given at birth. It only came to mean a person of natural intelligence or talent in the seventeenth century. The synonymous term brilliant has a different origin, related more closely to the history of colors and art. The meaning we use and understand today, sparkling, shining, incandescent, comes from the French brilliant, as recorded in the 1680s. This meaning, however, comes from the Latin *beryllus* and the Greek *bēryllos*, referring to the mineral beryl (beryllium)—a semiprecious stone whose more famous varieties include emerald and aquamarine. The connotations of being admirable and exceptional come from the nineteenth century, while its use of diamonds was first recorded in Venice in the seventeenth century.

In terms of art, this insight into etymology has a few points of interest to us. On the one hand, the mineral beryl in its purest form is colorless. Other substances (i.e., colors) are considered impurity (not unlike how Wittgenstein referred to black) the dirtying quality of black. In Medieval Latin, the term *berillus* was applied to any kind of pale green precious stone or crystal.

Eventually, it played a role in the naming of glasses or spectacles German die Brille, "spectacles." This brings us to a correlation between brilliance and seeing, or seeing clearly.

On the other hand, even a superficial overview of art history will take us from the German Brille to Brillo, albeit not for Andy Warhol's statement with his *Brillo Boxes*, but for their original content, which was soap pads. While we may prefer to consider brilliance as connected to purity of mind, exceptional brightness, and luminosity, rather than washing our dishes, it helps to have this excellent example of marketing in mind as well. As Roland Barthes has shown us in his *Mythologies*, the linguistics of daily life and the advertising industry sometimes provide us with deep and meaningful insight into otherwise complex phenomena.

From antiquity and Medieval German languages, from the Venetian court to 1960s pop culture, we have been obsessing over ideas of cleanliness and clarity and the absence of impurities. The color black has often been seen as a factor of contamination (in Wittgenstein's terms, once mixed in, it decreases the brightness of any other color), darkness, and the unknown (Plato's Cave, being kept in the dark). We have normalized excluding it from the repertoire of "official" colors and considering it as a total absence of light, a *noncolor*. We use light as a metaphor for knowledge and truth (enlightenment), and darkness plays a role in our description of all things unknown, intimidating, and backward.

And yes, we use black as a means of clarification as well, of imbuing with meaning seemingly pure white surfaces. Since the beginnings of our visual culture, black has been present—in the use of ash and charcoal on cave walls, in Chinese ink on woodblock, oil on linen, and ballpoint pen on paper. We have been sullying the tabula rasa with all of the different connotations and layers of meaning black has to offer. This much is apparent even in the dimmest of lights and darkest of circumstances, and this is the true brilliance of the so-called noncolor: black.

INDEX

D

E

Z